Drug Court Justice

NEW PERSPECTIVES
IN CRIMINOLOGY
AND CRIMINAL JUSTICE

Jeffrey Ian Ross
General Editor

Vol. 4

PETER LANG
New York • Washington, D.C./Baltimore • Bern
Frankfurt am Main • Berlin • Brussels • Vienna • Oxford

Kevin Whiteacre

Drug Court Justice

Experiences in a Juvenile Drug Court

PETER LANG
New York • Washington, D.C./Baltimore • Bern
Frankfurt am Main • Berlin • Brussels • Vienna • Oxford

Library of Congress Cataloging-in-Publication Data

Whiteacre, Kevin.
Drug court justice: experiences in a juvenile drug court / Kevin Whiteacre.
p. cm. — (New perspectives in criminology and criminal justice; v. 4)
Includes bibliographical references.
1. Juvenile justice, Administration of. 2. Juvenile courts. 3. Drug courts.
4. Juvenile delinquents—Drug use. 5. Youth—Drug abuse. I. Title.
HV9069.W4228   345.73'02770269—dc22   2008003298
ISBN 978-1-4331-0056-7
ISSN 1555-3418

Bibliographic information published by **Die Deutsche Bibliothek**.
Die Deutsche Bibliothek lists this publication in the "Deutsche
Nationalbibliografie"; detailed bibliographic data is available
on the Internet at http://dnb.ddb.de/.

Cover design by Joni Holst

The paper in this book meets the guidelines for permanence and durability
of the Committee on Production Guidelines for Book Longevity
of the Council of Library Resources.

© 2008 Peter Lang Publishing, Inc., New York
29 Broadway, 18th floor, New York, NY 10006
www.peterlang.com

Printed in the United States of America

TABLE OF CONTENTS

TABLES

FOREWORD

Due to the war on drugs, the modern state—specifically the judicial system—has been forced to devise new and seemingly benign ways to deal with lawbreakers. One of the most recently developed methods of doing so is the drug court. At face value, drug courts have a number of advantages. They are designed to prevent otherwise law-abiding citizens from going to jail or prison; concentrate expertise in the judicial field; and, in the end, hopefully mandate or coerce "offenders" into some kind of rehabilitative program.

This type of sanction was almost unimaginable two decades ago. Meanwhile, drug courts have been touted as a panacea for all that ails the clogged criminal courts and criminal justice system in America. It is no wonder that this practice has expanded beyond adult courts to juvenile courts as well. The drug court phenomenon has transformed not only the ideas of justice and sanctions, but also the role of therapy in rehabilitation. Additionally, the pains and gains of drug courts are felt by the accused as well as by their parents, court workers, and case managers.

Drug courts have altered both the way that justice is meted out and the kinds and means of sanctions we impose on lawbreakers. Unfortunately, despite the huge investment by our federal and state governments, there is little rigorous research on this topic. The minimal work that has been conducted reflects some very real and serious limitations.

As the editor of Peter Lang's series "New Perspectives in Criminology and Criminal Justice," I'm happy to introduce readers to Kevin Whiteacre's in-depth study, *Drug Court Justice: Experiences in a Juvenile Drug Court.* Like the two preceding books in this series, Whiteacre's book offers respectable, cutting-edge scholarship that pushes the boundaries of the disciplines of criminology and criminal justice.

Drug Court Justice analyzes a number of important issues, especially the day-to-day experiences of juvenile drug-court participants (i.e., offenders, their probation officers, attorneys, parents, judges and other court workers). He also looks at the dynamics of case processing and peripheral controls to which juvenile drug-court offenders are exposed, including the all-pervasive urine tests. Finally, Whiteacre focuses on how juvenile drug courts can have an effect on the wider society.

I'm sure that scholars, instructors, practitioners, and students in many fields—not just those of criminology, criminal justice, anthropology, and sociology—will be intrigued by Whiteacre's book.

Jeffrey Ian Ross, Ph.D.

ACKNOWLEDGMENTS

I would like to express my sincere gratitude to Professors Steve Chermak, Ed McGarrell, Phil Parnell, and Steve Russell for their helpful comments on earlier drafts of this manuscript. Special thanks to Hal Pepinsky for his comments, support, and encouragement during the initial research. Thanks to the JDC staff and treatment counselors for their honesty and openness, and thanks to the juveniles for sharing their experiences with me. I would also like to thank Liz, the love of my life, for tirelessly reviewing this manuscript again and again.

Many thanks to Jeffrey Ian Ross, Editor for Peter Lang's "New Perspectives in Criminology and Criminal Justice" series, for his kind words and very helpful suggestions for tightening up the manuscript. Thanks also to Phyllis Korper, Senior Editor for Peter Lang, for accepting the book for publication, to begin with. Finally, I owe a debt of gratitude to Daniel Abrahamson and the Hon. Morris Hoffman for agreeing to review the book and for their support and kind words.

1 | INTRODUCTION

The growth of the drug court movement has been fast and phe-
nomenal. Combining the hopes of rehabilitation with the promise
of punishment, the drug court model requires individuals arrested
on drug charges to attend treatment and regularly scheduled court
hearings and undergo periodical drug tests. A system of graduated
sanctions rewards participants for compliance and punishes them
for noncompliance. After successful completion, the participants
may have their charges dropped or reduced.

In 1989, the first adult drug treatment court opened in Dade
County (Miami), Florida. More than 1,500 adult, juvenile, and
tribal drug courts are operating in the United States and its territories. Thousands of people have participated in these programs,
and tens of millions of federal dollars have poured into them. Drug
courts have been implemented in Europe, Canada, and Australia
as well.

Unfortunately, the speed of growth has outstripped professional research attempts to assess their impacts. The studies that
do exist tend to focus on rearrest rates or an occasional cost-
efficiency analysis based on those recidivism rates. Few, if any,
consider other possible effects associated with drug court practices
on the participants or the implications of those practices for society
in general except the possibility that they may slightly reduce rearrests for drug use or other offenses. Fewer rearrests are clearly
good for the participants (if only for practical reasons), but evaluations must also include other possible consequences associated

with coerced abstinence equally important to the participants' lives and to society in general.

This book embarks on an exploratory study of a juvenile drug treatment court (the JDC) in the Midwest. It investigates how denial, surveillance, coercion, accountability, and definitions of success operate and interact in the JDC environment and become intertwined with institutional needs and authority structures. These themes emerged from my five years of experience in the field evaluating drug treatment courts, talking with participants and staff, and reading the research literature.

They represent some of the more contentious issues on drug courts specifically and, more generally, the rehabilitative ideal, coerced drug treatment, increasing levels of surveillance, and the growth of intermediate sanctions.

What Is a Drug Court?

Specific drug court program components vary among jurisdictions, but certain elements are common enough to constitute a template of sorts. Drug courts combine intensive court oversight with case management, treatment, and other social services to break the purported link between drug abuse and crime. The drug court judge works with prosecutors, defense attorneys, probation officers, and drug treatment specialists to "require appropriate treatment for offenders, monitor their progress, and ensure the delivery of other services, like education or job skills training, to help offenders remain crime and drug-free" (National Association of Drug Court Professionals, 1997). The drug court template, therefore, is characterized by the redefined roles among staff, the focus on drug using offenders, and a new process of court-driven treatment.

Staff

One aspect of this court innovation is a change in the roles of the courtroom workgroup. Drug court judges play the role of team captain, taking on a more expansive role than regular court duties require (United States General Accounting Office [USGAO], 1995). In addition to the traditional responsibilities the judge assumes, including presiding over hearings and issuing bench warrants, the drug court judge presides over prehearing treatment progress meetings and drug court compliance hearings, sanctions or terminates participants from the program, and in some cases adjudicates new criminal charges (Goldkamp, 1994).

During the hearings, the judge acts as a counselor, praising successes and reprimanding failures. As one drug court judge put it, "We pat some people on the back, we slap some people on the rump. We hug some people, literally, and some people we chastise. But it's all for the purpose of making sure that everybody who is here has some understanding that the purpose is all the same" (quoted in Nolan, 2001, p. 71). Much is made of the drug court judge's new role and the unique powers of a judge's chastisement and encouragement to help reform an offender.

Public defenders and prosecutors also redefine their traditional adversarial roles, cooperating in the courtroom to help participants succeed in the program. In the treatment courtroom, the prosecutor will often both encourage participants who are complying and threaten with prosecution those who are not (Goldkamp, 1994). Meanwhile, the defense attorney plays a role that "appears more therapeutic in nature than adversarial" (p. 114). Often, this role entails trying to keep the participant in treatment until program graduation and even counseling a client to disclose continued drug use (Hora, Schma, & Rosenthal, 1999).

Other players provide their traditional services. For example, social workers and/or probation officers may make house calls to check on participants, manage the drug testing responsibilities, and sometimes bring in uncooperative participants who have not shown up to treatment or court. Treatment personnel also go to court sessions and provide updates on each participant's progress in the program. They often manage cases, supervise treatment, and help decide when participants are ready to move through phases of treatment.

Participants

Juvenile drug treatment courts generally accept juveniles from 12 to 18 years of age. Most focus on juveniles 15 years of age or older (Cooper & Bartlett, 1998). The eligibility criteria for program participation vary. Foremost, arrested juveniles should present a substance abuse problem as defined by the program. A current drug offense is generally accepted by drug courts as prima facie evidence of a drug problem. Participants most often face current charges for drug possession offenses or other nonviolent offenses such as property crimes (USGAO, 1995). Some adult drug courts accept only first-time felony drug offenders.

Eligible offenses in juvenile drug treatment courts can range from alcohol possession (e.g., Yavapai-Apache Jurisdiction, Arizona) to any nonviolent felony or serious misdemeanor where the juvenile is using drugs, including alcohol (e.g., Pima County, Arizona), to "all nonviolent drug motivated offenses" (e.g., Duval County, Florida) (Office of Justice Programs [OJP], 2001). Most juvenile and adult drug courts will not accept defendants with prior convictions for violent crimes or current charges for violent offenses. In an effort to distinguish between drug users and dealers, many courts also stipulate maximum amounts of drugs with which the defendant can be caught to qualify for the program.

For juvenile drug courts nationally, the level of participants' previous contacts with the criminal justice system varies across jurisdictions. In Albuquerque, New Mexico, participants averaged 6.5 prior arrests, and in Missoula, Montana, they averaged 10.1 prior charges.[1] On the other hand, many juvenile participants in other jurisdictions (e.g., Beckham County, Oklahoma, and Orange County, Florida) are first or second time offenders (Belenko, 2001). Nationally, more than 80 percent of participants have had at least one prior criminal justice contact (Belenko, 2001).

Most juvenile drug court participants are male (over 80 percent). Caucasians account for almost half of the participants. African Americans and Hispanics comprise just less than a quarter each, and other races, including Asian/Pacific Islanders and Native Americans, make up about another 5 percent.

The Process

Though programs differ, juvenile drug courts can be broken into two basic phases: stabilization and aftercare. The first phase, stabilization, includes the assessment of participants' needs and the initial intake. In this phase, participants are under intensive monitoring from the court through regularly scheduled compliance hearings, drug tests, and treatment meetings. Programs usually require attendance in court every two to four weeks. At these meetings, the judge reviews the participant's progress in treatment and any drug test results.

The court uses progressive sanctions to motivate offenders toward program success (Deschenes & Greenwood, 1994). Violations of program rules and requirements are met with sanctions of increasing severity, from verbal admonition by the judge, required attendance at more status hearings, demotion to the previous treatment phase, required additional drug tests, and community service to short-term incarceration and ultimately termination from the program followed by criminal proceedings (USGAO, 1995). The judge can also issue rewards for success such as verbal praise, fewer status hearings, and promotion to the next treatment phase.

Participants must also attend treatment meetings, usually counseling sessions provided through a contracted treatment agency. Some programs may also require attendance at Alcoholics Anonymous or Narcotics Anonymous meetings. A few even include "alternative interventions, including wilderness experiences, acupuncture, and animal therapy" (Butts & Roman, 2004).

The next phase, aftercare, concentrates on maintaining the participants' changes. It is less intensive than the first, and the number of required drug tests and compliance hearings is reduced. Relapse is an expected and common occurrence in the program, so a participant may move back and forth through the phases or be held in one for an extended time period, depending on the number and extent of problems. Finally, when a participant successfully completes the program, by fulfilling program obligations by remaining arrest- and drug-free for a specified time span, attending treatment meetings and court hearings, and so on, and graduates from the program, the court may dismiss the original charge, reduce or set aside a sentence, offer some lesser penalty, or offer a combination of these (National Association of Drug Court Professionals, 1997).

The Drug Court Boom

The "War on Drugs" and the attendant increase in the arrest, prosecution, and incarceration of drug users over the past 25 years has put a considerable strain on the American criminal justice system. During the 1980s, drug arrests more than doubled (from 580,900 in 1980 to 1,361,700 in 1989) (Bureau of Justice Statistics [BJS], 2007a). From 1980 to 2005, drug arrests more than tripled, reaching 1,846,351 in 2005 (about 5,058 drug arrests a day or an arrest almost every 17 seconds). Drug arrests currently constitute more than 30 percent of all arrests. In 2005, about 80 percent of all drug arrests were possession offenses; over a third of those arrests were for possession of marijuana (BJS, 2007b).[2]

Meanwhile, in the increasingly punitive antidrug climate of the 1980s, spurred in part by the emergence and spread of crack cocaine, prosecutors became less willing to divert drug cases out of the court system. The huge increase in arrests coupled with this reluctance to divert opened the "floodgates to the courts" (Lipscher, 1989). A study of 17 urban trial courts, for example, found that between 1983 and 1987 drug caseloads increased by 56 percent (Goerdt & Martin, 1989). This flood of drug cases caused serious backlogs in the court system, threatening the operations and stability of some courts.

> [T]he potential benefits of traditional delay reduction strategies had been exhausted, existing procedures could not be streamlined further to accommodate the surging drug caseloads, the existing case management system could not be worked any harder, and the traditional case disposition process could not keep pace with the volume of cases generated by this aggressive law enforcement strategy. (Cooper & Trotter, 1994, p. 84)

To avert an impending judicial crisis, court officials began experimenting with new case management strategies. They responded with a range of changes from simpler techniques like early disposition and consolidation of drug cases to other bolder methods like specialized expedited drug courts. Court officials began to feel, however, that many of these strategies failed to address the needs of drug-dependent defendants (Cooper & Trotter, 1994). Court staff noticed the same defendants were coming through court repeatedly, and expedition just made the revolving door swing faster. Some specialized drug courts then changed goals from speeding up disposition to treating the arrested drug users, by providing court managed drug treatment.

Court officials in Dade County created the first adult drug treatment court in 1989. Planners based this new court on the idea that reducing the demand for drugs would reduce drug-related crimes. Though courts had often assigned treatment to defendants as a stipulation of their probation sentence, the Dade County Drug Court became the first to actually integrate the expertise of the treatment providers with the leadership of the judiciary to offer a rigorous court-ordered treatment program for drug using offenders

(Goldkamp, 1993, 1994). Soon after, other jurisdictions began implementing their own versions of drug treatment courts.

Between 1991 and 1993, more than 20 jurisdictions across the country implemented drug courts (Goldkamp, 1994). By 1999, there were 349 adult drug courts, and by 2006 a total of 906 adult drug courts had been implemented (Bureau of Justice Assistance [BJA] Drug Court Clearinghouse, 2006). Adult drug courts are now in all 50 states, the District of Columbia, and some American territories, as well as Australia, Canada, England, Ireland, and Scotland (Nolan, 2002). There are reentry drug courts, tribal drug courts, and family drug courts (Huddleston, Freeman-Wilson, Marlowe, & Roussell, 2005). The National Association of Drug Court Professionals has grown to represent over 16,000 drug court professionals and community leaders (Huddleston et al., 2005).

In 1995, the first juvenile and family drug treatment courts opened (Cooper & Bartlett, 1998). The growth of juvenile drug treatment courts stemmed from the adult drug court movement and was similarly spurred by increases in juvenile arrests for alcohol and drug-related arrests (though not necessarily increases in actual usage).

According to the Uniform Crime Reports, 1.8 million juveniles (persons under the age of 18) were arrested in 1995—the year of the first juvenile drug court—an overall increase of 30 percent from 1986 (Federal Bureau of Investigation [FBI], 1995). During that same time juvenile arrests for drug offenses increased 115 percent. Arrests for curfew violations and gambling offenses also increased substantially.

Data from the University of Michigan's Monitoring the Future Study, however, indicate that juveniles' patterns of recent drug and alcohol use (any use at least once within 30 days of the survey) did not necessarily coincide with those increasing arrest rates. Recent use of alcohol among tenth graders, for example, changed little in the 1990s (42.8 percent in 1991; 40.1 percent in 1997; 33.8 percent in 2006). Though there was a considerable decline in marijuana use from 1980 to 1992, it rose from 8.1 percent in 1992 to 20.5 percent in 1997 and came down to 14.2 percent in 2006. Use of other illicit drugs has continued to remain relatively low (6.3 percent in 2006—inhalants, such as spray paint, comprise the bulk of this group).

In 2000, there were 172 juvenile drug courts; by 2006 there were 411 (BJA Drug Court Clearing House, 2006). Thousands of juveniles have processed through drug courts. Colorado State University, with the help of $350,000 from the U.S. Department of Education's Safe and Drug Free Schools program, implemented the nation's first college drug treatment court for students accused of campus drug and alcohol violations.

A large infusion of federal funds to jurisdictions catalyzed the development and implementation of adult and juvenile drug courts. From fiscal year 1995 through 1997, the Drug Courts Program Office (DCPO) awarded approximately 270 jurisdictions more than $47 million in drug court grants. Its appropriations for fiscal years 1997 and 1998 were $30 million each (Hoffman, 2000). The National Drug Control Strategy earmarked $50 million for 2001 and 2002 each, and for 2003 the amount was raised to $52 million (Office of National Drug Control Policy [ONDCP], 2002). In 2005, the Department of Justice (DOJ) awarded $25 million in grants to "plan, implement, or improve drug courts." The support of this substantial finding from these government sources helped cultivate the popularity of drug courts in many jurisdictions.

Therapeutic Jurisprudence

The drug policy crisis that overwhelmed the courts provided the *structural* impetus for the drug court movement, but there were also coinciding "cultural currents that justified, informed, and gave meaning to the advent of this judicial innovation" (Nolan, 2001, p. 49). Punishment practices reflect a society's "sensibility and symbolic themes" as much as they represent a response to structural needs (Garland, 1990). It is no coincidence, then, that drug courts emerged around the same time that the therapeutic jurisprudence perspective emerged in legal scholarship (Nolan, 2001; Furedi, 2002). In fact, some proponents have argued that drug courts represent a "significant step in the evolution of therapeutic jurisprudence—the evolutionary step from theory to practice" (Hora et al., 1999, p. 448). A brief discussion of therapeutic jurisprudence and its roots, therefore, seems appropriate for this introduction.

Therapeutic jurisprudence arguably represents a new twist to turn-of-the-century sociological jurisprudence, which was concerned with identifying the actual *effects* of the law on the society, and the concomitant Progressive social movement.[3] Proponents of sociological jurisprudence, such as Roscoe Pound and Joseph Bingham, sought to incorporate the relatively new social sciences into analyses of the actual impacts of judicial decisions and rules of law. They criticized the formalism of traditional jurisprudence that sought to identify the "proper" law or legal principle and apply it to a specific case while ignoring the actual consequences of a legal decision (G. E. White, 1972).

Advocates suggested that the legal profession depend on other fields to evaluate the effects of legal decisions (G. E. White, 1972). Expert interpretation of empirical phenomena by professionals in other "scientific" fields, such as sociology and economics, they believed, could help legal actors make their institutions more responsive to the unique conditions and needs of twentieth-century America. Judges could replace the "illusory certainty of legal rules" with the "reasonable and just solutions of individual cases" (p. 1005).

Similarly, modern-day therapeutic jurisprudence "seeks to apply social science to examine law's impact on the mental and physical health of the people it affects" (Winick, 1997, p. 3). Therapeutic jurisprudence evaluates law, substantive rules, legal procedures, the actions of legal professionals, and governmental policies by the extent to which they encourage therapeutic or antitherapeutic outcomes. Characterized by a scientifically based approach to identifying the therapeutic impacts of laws, it can, according to proponents, serve as a tool to frame a new research agenda. All laws have potentially therapeutic and antitherapeutic effects. Proponents of therapeutic jurisprudence argue for including consideration of these effects in any evaluation of legal practices and policies. Research in the therapeutic jurisprudence vein has included analyses of the side effects of incompetency labeling, the right to refuse treatment, the implications of labeling individuals as dangerous, coerced treatment, and drug courts (see Wexler & Winick, 1991; Winick, 1997).

Research Issues

The Early Years

Despite the rapid spread of drug courts and the large sums of money appropriated, early reports of their effects were generally limited to anecdotal evidence or in-house evaluations by employees of the drug courts (Nolan, 2001; Rossman, Butts, Roman, DeStefano, & White, 2004). These early in-house evaluations often reported substantial decreases in recidivism for participants (or just the graduates), which bolstered the image of drug courts and their success rates, but external evaluations rarely supported these claims (Nolan, 2001). In fact, one of the first formal impact studies of a drug court (Dade County), found no significant difference in one-year recidivism rates between defendants sentenced before drug court implementation (33 percent) and defendants adjudicated after DTC implementation (32 percent) (Smith & American Bar Association, 1991, cited in Hoffman, 2002).

Overall, early peer-reviewed outcome studies presented disparate results. Some reported reductions in recidivism, while others showed little difference at all (Belenko, 1999; Hoffman, 2000), and at least one reported increased rates of recidivism (Miethe, Lu, & Reese, 2000). In 1997, the USGAO (now the U.S. Government Accountability Office) completed a metastudy of 20 drug treatment court evaluations produced by 16 jurisdictions. It found that 14 of the 20 studies used no comparison between participants' and non-participants' arrest rates after program completion. Ultimately, the USGAO (1997) concluded that the data did not permit any "definitive conclusions concerning overall impact of drug courts" (p. 13). The USGAO (2002) recommended steps the DOJ could take to improve "the methodological soundness of future federally funded impact evaluations" (p. 1). Foremost, it suggested collecting data on participants' criminal recidivism and postprogram follow-up data on drug use relapse "to the extent possible."

Shortly after the USGAO report, Steven Belenko (1998) analyzed 30 drug court evaluation reports covering 24 drug courts, including 4 juvenile drug courts. He concluded that drug courts do retain offenders in long-term treatment and other services and reduce recidivism (generally measured as rearrest and time to re-arrest) among participants. Few of the outcome studies, how-ever, provided both adequate descriptions of the comparison groups and found statistically significant decreases in recidivism (Belenko, 1998). Most compared the entire control (nondrug court) group with only the drug court graduates, eliminating the more trouble-some drug court participants from that group and inflating the apparent success (Belenko, 1998).

Belenko (1999) then published another review of 29 evaluation reports covering 30 drug courts, including 4 juvenile drug courts in 1999. The Fairfield County Ohio juvenile drug court reported a 21 percent recidivism rate for participants but provided no other recidivism information for a control group. An evaluation of a Utah juvenile drug court indicated a greater reduction in overall, misdemeanor, and alcohol or drug arrests for drug court participants than for a matched control group. It did not provide evidence of statistical significance. The two other juvenile drug court evaluations provided no postprogram analyses (Belenko, 1999).

In 2002, the USGAO published a follow-up report to its 1997 study to assess improvements in data collection for national impact studies. The report was titled clearly enough, *Drug Courts: Better DOJ Data Collection and Evaluation Efforts Needed to Measure Impact of Drug Court Programs.* The USGAO summed up their findings, "DOJ continues to lack vital information that the Congress, the public, and other program stakeholders may need to determine the overall impact of federally funded drug court programs and to assess whether drug court programs are an effective use of federal funds" (USGAO, 2002, p. 3).

Remarkably, the USGAO (2002) reported that the DCPO, an office within the Department of Justice's OJP, which provides grant funds to and has had oversight responsibilities for more than 500 drug courts, had, in 2000, actually eliminated survey questions intended to collect postprogram outcome data from the programs to which it provides funds (p. 12). According to the DCPO director, drug court grantees claimed they were unable to provide postprogram outcome data and lacked sufficient resources to do so. In its report, however, the GAO questioned this decision by the DCPO and its claim that collecting outcome data was not feasible (USGAO, 2002, p. 12).

The Cream of the Crop

The most persistent and widespread methodological problem in both adult and juvenile drug court research has been the use of improper comparison groups. To demonstrate reduced recidivism among drug court participants, an outcome study should compare the experimental group of all drug court participants to a control group of similarly situated offenders following a nondrug court track of adjudication like regular probation.

The majority of drug court recidivism studies, however, compare only the successful graduates of a drug court (sometimes only about half of the total number of participants), eliminating the drug court participants who left the program unsuccessfully but retaining the entire control group for the final analysis. Some evaluations, lacking an external control group, actually compare the successful, and most compliant/motivated, drug court graduates with the unsuccessful, less compliant/motivated drug court participants (Belenko, 1998).

Such "skimming" of the experimental group, eliminating the poorly performing or less compliant participants from the drug court group, while leaving everyone in the control group (or even constructing the control group entirely of the noncompliant participants eliminated from the original experimental group), grossly inflates the apparent success of drug courts.[4] Breaking up the experimental group allows too many extraneous unmeasured variables, like participant motivation, compliance, treatment readiness, and so on, to enter the model, rendering the study uninformative at best. Both the experimental and control groups contain motivated and unmotivated, compliant and noncompliant, more criminal and less criminal participants, those who are more employable and less employable, and so on, but the skimming method excludes the more problematic individuals from the drug court group while leaving them in the control group. It is like evaluating two high schools by comparing the test scores of only the honors students from one school against the test scores for the entire student body of the other.[5]

As a consequence, the early research models used for evaluating drug courts, like those the USGAO consistently identified, were not just a random scattering of different methodological problems. Rather they were improper research designs that systematically biased outcomes toward showing positive effects of drug courts.

Researchers with the Urban Institute sum up the situation well:

> Of course evaluations do not always produce useful evidence of program impact. Funding agencies place great pressure on drug courts to demonstrate efficacy, and it is not surprising that some evaluation protocols are biased toward positive program outcomes. For example, it is very common for drug courts to test their effectiveness by comparing the recidi-

vism of program graduates with the recidivism of nongraduates or youth removed from drug court as a result of noncompliance. Clearly, these groups are not comparable, and under these conditions the effect of the drug court process cannot be disentangled from basic underlying differences between the groups. Evaluations of this type have helped promote drug courts as a promising program model, but they have not provided high-quality evidence of impact. (Roman & DeStefano, 2004, p. 109)

This method is widely regarded as wrong (Goldkamp, White, & Robinson, 2001; Roman & DeStefano, 2004). Yet, studies employing it are still cited as evidence of drug court effectiveness. As an indication of how this improper method might be so widespread that it is establishing itself as the standard practice in drug court evaluations, Sanford and Arrigo (2005), in their review of drug court evaluations, actually qualify the findings of a study that found that drug court participants had higher recidivism rates than the control group with the caveat, "However, their analyses did not distinguish between drug court graduates and sample participants who may or may not have successfully completed the program" (p. 242). Sanford and Arrigo implicitly criticize the findings because the study did *not* skim the experimental group.

It's Getting Better

Importantly, not all studies suffer from such problems, and some of the small "handful of more rigorous evaluations," using more appropriate samples, has demonstrated reductions in recidivism and drug use among drug court participants (Gottfredson, Najaka, & Kearley, 2003).[6]

In 2005, the USGAO completed a third metastudy of drug courts. Out of 117 drug court evaluations they considered, 27 (23 percent) were chosen for review because they met the USGAO's criteria for "methodological soundness."[7] This time, the USGAO concluded that the research did indeed provide some evidence of reduced recidivism among drug court participants for a length of time roughly equal to that of the drug court program.

Studies of adult and juvenile drug courts in Ohio, likewise, have found that drug court participants as a group, appropriately defined as all those individuals who participated in the drug court, were less likely to be rearrested than the comparison groups during the follow-up period (Latessa, Listwan, Shaffer, Lowenkamp, & Ratansi, 2001; Latessa, Shaffer, & Lowenkamp, 2002). A review of six drug courts in Washington state found significant reductions in recidivism among participants in five of the courts (Washington State Institute for Public Policy, 2003). Slowly, a body of good research is beginning to suggest that adult and juvenile drug courts can have a moderate impact on recidivism and drug use.[8]

Besides general outcome studies of programs, researchers are beginning to look at the effects of specific program components on recidivism and drug use (Marlowe, 2004). For example, researchers are analyzing the effects of graduated sanctions for positive drug tests and judicial status hearings: "An alternative approach to assessing the efficacy of drug court is to evaluate the effects of manipulating its core ingredients. Demonstrating that judicial status hearings have a significant bearing on drug-court outcomes establishes that drug courts have a unique mechanism of action" (Marlowe, 2004).

This book represents one such attempt to critically analyze and better understand how the ingredients of a drug court—confrontation of denial, punishment for noncompliance, and surveillance through drug testing—are experienced in practice by the participants and staff involved in a juvenile drug court.

New Questions

If research unequivocally demonstrates that drug courts can decrease rates of recidivism and drug use among participants, many questions still remain regarding other impacts such coerced treatment may have on participants. All policies carry their own set of side effects (Kleiman, 1992). As Mark Kleiman writes, "Drugs sometimes cause damage. Good drug policy limits that damage, doing as little harm as possible in the process" (p. 12). The potential for untoward effects lurks in every policy.

Shuman (1996) notes that "[r]escue proceeds on the assumption that it will be therapeutic; we encourage rescue because we think it will be beneficial to the physical or emotional health of the person rescued" (p. 299). A court program that constrains individuals to a course of action "for their own good" arguably incurs a special responsibility to make sure that the treatment into which people are being coerced does, in fact, pose a reasonable expectation of benefit and little likelihood of harm (W. R. Miller, 1991). Wouldn't the logic of studying components to see "what works" imply we should also study them for possible untoward effects?[9] What doesn't work, and what does it even mean to *work*?

A considerable limitation of prior drug court research is the narrow focus on abstinence and recidivism as the sole measure of program success.[10] While certainly important, these two outcomes represent a small part of the myriad outcomes experienced in a drug court program. This limited view has left a gulf between the rhetoric of drug treatment courts and the lived experiences of those individuals participating in and staffing the programs. Or, to appropriate what Joan Petersilia (2003) said of parole, "the devil is not in the principle but in the details" (p. 17).

This book is concerned with some of the details, and the principles underlying them, that have been largely left out of the discussions of drug courts and their effects. In particular, the variables that most interested me were denial, sanctions, and surveillance. Through my own observations of a juvenile drug court and interviews with the adolescents and staff, I investigated how issues of denial, coercion, surveillance, and definitions of success operate and interact in a juvenile drug treatment court environment. The findings presented here raise some serious questions about the effects of juvenile drug court practices.

The Book

The discussion is presented within the context of three primary themes: (1) denial and the nonadversarial court; (2) coercing treatment compliance; and (3) drug testing and surveillance. These topics represent distinct but interrelated components of the JDC, and drug courts generally. They are the processes of the court. They can be thought of as new variables, whose values will be assessed through interviews with JDC court staff, treatment counselors, and the participants themselves. Relevant literature is also brought in to supplement the insights gained from the interviews.

Chapter 2 describes the JDC and its population. Generally, the JDC and its participants are similar to juvenile drug courts nationwide. Most were arrested for marijuana possession, and some have had prior experience with the criminal justice system. Interestingly, few were diagnosed as drug dependent. Most were identified as "abusers." Some were also found to have behavioral disorders such as Attention Deficit Hyperactivity Disorder (ADHD) or Oppositional Defiance.

Chapter 3 explores the meaning of denial for youth and program staff and how it operates in the JDC. In drug courts, denial is a pervasive issue in both the legal procedures of the court and in drug treatment itself. The youths were by and large rather ambivalent toward their drug use, the program, and its staff. This ambivalence often resulted in resistance to the staff members' definitions of them as drug abusers. For some of the staff, denial was just a part of being young, and the juveniles' resistance to their views of drug abuse simply provided more evidence of the youths' denial.

Rather than an objective, independently existing condition, denial is the product of social interactions and ultimately reflects disagreement between two or more parties. As such, the attribution of denial is left to the subjective judgments of the authorities running the program. Finally, the court's articulation of denial within a legal setting enables it to maintain the staff's goals and definitions, insulating the program from dissent and legitimizing it.

Chapters 4 and 5 address the court's use of punishment to ensure compliance with treatment requirements. Much of the popularity of drug courts lies in their marriage of punishment and treatment ideologies. This marriage is so complete that proponents do not even see punishments for noncompliance as punishments. They are rather "adjustments" or "therapeutic responses."

Nevertheless, things are a bit more complicated in practice. Staff often disagreed about appropriate levels of punishments and whether they were harsh enough—evidence that punishments may still indeed be punishments. More importantly, staff members had contradictory views about the efficacy of punishments, particularly when faced with juveniles who remained noncompliant despite the punishments. They neutralized this internal tension by concluding that the punishments could only help those who wanted to be helped, creating a paradox for coercion, which is meant to be used specifically on those who do *not* want to comply. In the end, it was all resolved through the notion of accountability, which justified retributive punishments of transgressions simply because they were transgressions. What remains unanswered is whether the punishments actually enhance therapeutic outcomes or if staff even expects them to.

Chapter 6 explores the growing reliance on drug testing in the drug court as well as the criminal justice system and wider society. As drug tests become more technologically advanced, cheaper, and easier to use, they are becoming an increasingly important component of the drug court approach. Drug tests are used to monitor participants for drug use; they serve as punishments for noncompliance; they are outcome measures of drug court "success"; and for some staff, they are regarded as sufficient for the drug court program in and of themselves.

Some of the juveniles report that drug tests do indeed help keep them off drugs, and the staff certainly believes it. This chapter suggests, however, that the increasing reliance on drug tests might be driven by technology more than any demonstrated therapeutic benefits. In other words, treatment is being shaped by advances in surveillance technologies more than technology is responding to treatment needs. The chapter also situates the growth of drug testing within a broader reorientation of society toward surveillance, information collection, and classification. Finally, some possible implications of this trend for treatment and the larger society are considered.

Chapter 7 discusses staff and juveniles' definitions of successful outcomes. Despite the often critical observations made in the book, many of the juveniles did indeed often report benefits from the JDC, and the staff certainly felt they helped them. These benefits include, most importantly, getting their charges expunged, as well as reducing their drug use, improving in school, and getting along better with friends and family.

Finally, Chapter 8 considers the potential net-widening effect of the growth of juvenile drug courts and questions whether the current intensive approach is appropriate for nondependent marijuana smokers. In light of the findings, I make some suggestions for reforming the juvenile drug court approach, informed by harm reduction. These suggestions include client-driven treatment, focusing on the problems the youths identify themselves, and letting go of abstinence as a necessary outcome. The question remains whether the criminal justice system, with its tendency toward legalistic definitions of drug abuse and its reliance on punishment and surveillance as treatment tools, is the most efficacious environment for providing therapeutic programming.

The Appendix provides a description of the methods I used to conduct the research, including descriptions of the study sample and the interviews and observations that provide my data and upon which I base my arguments and draw my conclusions.

2 | THE JUVENILE DRUG COURT

The JDC is located in a Midwestern metropolitan jurisdiction. It was started in the early 2000s in response to growing drug-related cases in the area. Over the past decade and a half, the county's Juvenile Court, like many others across the country, had seen felony and misdemeanor drug arrests increase rather dramatically. When submitting its application for a federal grant to start the JDC, the court reported that more than 1,000 juvenile drug and alcohol cases had been filed in 1998—up from over a dozen total cases for possession of a controlled substance in 1985. Not surprisingly, the jurisdiction also reported that 50 percent of the juveniles brought to the county's detention center were testing positive for drug use—as would be expected, regardless of actual drug use trends in the population, when there are more drug-related arrests.

This chapter describes the JDC where I conducted my observations and interviews. This includes a description of the population of program participants in the first year and those who agreed to participate in the study.

The Process

The JDC is a six-month program, consisting of two three-month phases. Phase 1 is more rigorous, requiring attendance at a compliance hearing once every two weeks, between one to three drug tests a week, and usually at least one group treatment meeting a week. Phase 2 requires fewer drug tests, but if a youth is found noncompliant, more tests and other services can be ordered.

After a juvenile successfully completes the two phases and success-fully graduates, the court dismisses the charges that brought him or her into the program.

The JDC was intended for adolescents 12–17 years of age who face marijuana or alcohol-related charges or have a history of substance abuse (offenses involving violence are excluded). The eligibility list included youth who

1. face possession of marijuana charges,
2. have a history of substance abuse,
3. have a prior arrest for public intoxication or another alcohol-related charge,
4. are referred to the program by the prosecutor.

After arrest, the juveniles are screened for JDC eligibility. If deemed eligible, they attend an initial hearing with their parent(s) or guardian(s) at which time the judge goes over the responsibili-ties of the guardian and juvenile. The juveniles are then referred for a drug use assessment conducted by a privately contracted organization, separate from the contracted treatment provider, and the next court compliance hearing is scheduled. Once the assessment is completed, the juveniles begin attending the required treatment meetings and submitting urine samples for drug tests.

The juveniles in the JDC must attend regular mandatory com-pliance hearings at court every other week with at least one parent or legal guardian. In an effort to correspond with juveniles' and parents' work and school schedules, the hearings are held on a couple of nights during the week and on Saturday mornings. A drug test (urine sample) is taken at each court hearing.

On the night of the court compliance hearing, parents and juveniles wait in the waiting room outside the courtroom before it starts. When the hearing is to begin, they all come in together. At least one guardian must accompany the juvenile. Usually 5–12 juveniles are scheduled for an evening. The courtroom is small. It is quiet and carpeted. The gallery consists of four rows of about six wooden chairs in each row. The juveniles sit in the first two rows, so they can better observe what is happening. The guardians sit in the back two rows.

When a juvenile is called, he or she sits at the defense table with the accompanying guardian. If representing the juvenile, the public defender sits at the table as well, between them. The defender is present during all violation hearings when the juvenile may be expelled from the program. A typical hearing lasts only a few minutes for each juvenile.

After an extended period of compliance with treatment and court requirements, the juvenile may receive an "extension" as a reward. This extends the time period before the juvenile has to return for another compliance hearing, usually three to four weeks rather than two. In the second phase of treatment, juveniles who are in compliance need only come to court for an occasional drug test (for a minimum of 3 drug tests during the following 90 days). In Phase 2, participants do not have to attend compliance hearings, unless they violate conditions of the program. Their cases are set for administrative review at the end of Phase 2, where the judge dismisses the charges (to which the juvenile must admit guilt before entering the program) if the participants have successfully complied with the program requirements.

Entering the JDC

1. Eligibility
   – Youth is arrested.
   – Receiving office determines if youth is eligible for the program based on set criteria.
   – Urine screen is completed.
   – Coordinator provides information on the youth to the prosecutor who approves or denies program admittance within 24 hours.

2. Program Referral
   – JDC probation officer is given paperwork from screening.
   – Probation officer explains program to youth and parents.
   – If youth refuses to admit guilt, case is transferred to regular court within 48 hours.
   – Initial court hearing is set by screening.

3. Initial Hearing
   – Youth and parents/guardians hear legal rights and responsibilities on a video monitor in court waiting area.
   – Youth and parents/guardians are asked if they want legal representation.
   – Assessment time is set.
   – If youth refuses to admit guilt or participate in program, the case is sent to regular court within 24 hours.

Continued on next page.

4. JDC Program
- Youth and parent/guardian must attend biweekly compliance hearings in court.
- Drug tests are conducted at court hearings and treatment meetings.
- Youth and parent/guardian must check in with probation officer over phone to report on progress, school performance, and so on.
- Youth attends treatment counseling group meetings (usually once a week, depending on assessment).
- Probation officer occasionally checks in with school to check up on youth.

The majority of participants must attend weekly group treatment meetings with the privately contracted treatment provider once a week. The court contracts with one private treatment provider only. It uses funds from a federal grant to pay for both the treatment services and drug tests for participants.

After a positive drug test, a juvenile may get moved up to Intensive Outpatient, requiring two or three treatment meetings a week and an increase in drug tests. Sometimes a juvenile is assigned to additional outside meetings with Alcoholics Anonymous or Narcotics Anonymous.[11] The treatment group meetings also include individuals not associated with the JDC who are usually in treatment as a condition of probation. Most of the non-JDC treatment clients are there under some sort of criminal justice coercion.

The group treatment meetings are often broken up into two 50-minute meetings, one with juveniles only and the other combined with adults. The adults attend treatment as a condition of their probation, often for a drunk driving or possession offense. A few JDC juveniles, assessed as not having any drug problem, are not initially assigned to any treatment meetings—just court hearings and drug tests as long as their tests remain negative.

Every juvenile must attend one Alcohol and Drug Education class with at least one guardian. This is an eight-hour class offered one Saturday a month. In the class, a drug counselor provides a vast array of information about the dangers of drug use, using videos, lectures, and class discussions.

As mentioned, the court contracts with one treatment provider, but the participants can choose from among a number of branch offices, according to location convenience and other concerns. A treatment coordinator serves as the liaison between the treatment provider and the drug court. The coordinator attends court sessions and prehearing staff meetings, providing updates on each participant's progress in treatment. The updates include a record of participants' attendance at treatment meetings, participants' completion of the alcohol/drug education class, and other related information.

The frequency of drug testing at the JDC is largely determined by the counselors' recommendations. Testing may occur weekly, biweekly, or several times a week, depending upon the juvenile's assessment. The median time between drug tests was about 14 days.[12] Since marijuana was by far the most popular drug of choice, that seemed adequate, as it takes several weeks for the body to completely eliminate marijuana's metabolites. Overall, about 18 percent of the drug tests were positive—usually for marijuana. Only about 50 percent of the juveniles tested positive in their first test upon entering the program.

Drug Court Officials

The judge presides over the courtroom compliance hearings and the prehearing staff meetings. During the prehearing staff meetings, probation officers and the treatment liaison present information and recommendations to the judge. The prosecutor and the defender are present. The judge then decides on possible rewards or punishments, often contingent on how things go with the youth in the coming court hearing (e.g., the juvenile's cooperativeness, perceived honesty, or attitude). At the hearings, the judge also acts as a counselor of sorts, praising successes and reprimanding failures. One staffer said that the judge is "firm, yet the compassion is there." A juvenile described the judge as "hard but fair."

As with other drug courts, the public defender and prosecutor cooperate as a team to help the participants remain in the program. Other players provide their traditional services. Two or three probation officers manage the JDC cases at any one time. In the first year, two probation officers quit and were replaced. The probation officers' job is multifaceted. "It depends on the child and what the family calls for," a court staffer told me, "but they are to make sure the child does all the court orders. They're there to remind them. They make the referrals for community service work. They keep in contact with the counselors to make sure everyone is doing what they're supposed to be doing."

The probation officers in the JDC provide more intensive supervision of smaller caseloads than regular probation. The JDC officers average about 25 cases at a time compared to traditional probation's caseload of anywhere from 65 to 100 cases.[13] Whereas a regular probation officer might see a client once a month, JDC probation officers see them every other week, though quite briefly, during the regular compliance hearings in court. Parents and juveniles are also expected to call the probation officer once a week to check in and report how the juvenile is doing in school, any relapses in drug use, problems, and so on. The probation officers "have more contact with the juvenile than anybody in the courtroom," explained a staff member. "So their opinion is very important in the courtroom, because they're the ones who talk to [the juveniles]." Many of the juveniles, however, told me they often just leave a message on their probation officers' voice mail for their weekly update.

Participants

In its first year of operation, the JDC accepted around 177 juveniles into the program. Like juvenile drug courts nationally, the JDC's participants tended to be older youths (median = 15.5 years) (see Table 1). Just over half of the JDC participants were 16 years of age or older (less than 10 percent were only 12 or 13 years of age). About 80 percent of the participants were male. Female participants were on average almost a year younger than male participants. Almost two-thirds of the participants were Caucasian, just less than a third were African American, and about 4 percent were either Hispanic or biracial. Since the metropolitan area in which the court is located is roughly 85 percent Caucasian, 13 percent African American, and 1 percent Hispanic, this reflects an overrepresentation of African Americans within the criminal justice
system generally.

Table 1	Participant Characteristics
Participant Characteristics	(N=177)
Age	15.5 (mean)
	16.0 (median)

Continued on next page.

Race	(%)
Caucasian	63.3
African American	32.2
Other	4.4

Gender	(%)
Male	83.1
Female	16.9

Live With	(%)
Two Parents	42.5
Mother	40.3
Father	9.7
Extended Family	7.5

Less than half lived with two parents (including stepparents). The JDC participants are similar to juvenile drug court participants nationally in both gender and age. There are considerably fewer Hispanics, however, in the JDC than in other juvenile drug courts.

Consistent with the JDC eligibility requirements, possession of marijuana accounted for two-thirds of the complaints that brought the juveniles into the JDC (see Table 2). Possession of paraphernalia, public intoxication, and minor possession of alcohol made up most of the other charges. Many of the participants had multiple complaints for the same arrest (e.g., someone might have been picked up for both possession of marijuana and paraphernalia). So, there were also a few property charges and truancy offenses as well.

Juveniles in the JDC averaged 0.6 prior arrests. More than half had no prior arrests (technically, arrests are called "complaints" for the juveniles) when they entered the program. A few (less than 5 percent) had three or more prior arrests. The majority of these priors consisted of status offenses such as truancy or running away and some property offenses such as shoplifting. There were relatively few prior arrests for alcohol or other drugs. There were a few prior personal offenses such as intimidation or assault.

The juveniles had been arrested under many different circumstances. Some were smoking marijuana with friends outside in their neighborhood. One of the juveniles said he and a friend happened to have access to some marijuana growing outside. "I was in the neighborhood and me and my friend [were] actually just walking in the woods. I've seen it before on CDs and stuff, and I've smoked it before and stuff, so I knew what it looked like... People told me before it has to be a certain height, so I didn't know if it would be pickable or not, so we just picked it anyway. We went back to my friend's and dried it out... and went and smoked it. We did it in an abandoned house and got caught."

Table 2   Criminal Justice Information

Current Charges[a]	(%)
Possession of Marijuana	66.8
Possession of Paraphernalia	16.6
Alcohol Offense	6.6
Public Intoxication	5.8
Controlled Substance	1.2
Status	1.2
Property	0.8
Resisting Law	0.8
Number of Previous	0.6 (mean)
Arrests in JDC County	0.0 (median)
	(%)
0	58.8
1	28.2
2	10.2
3 or more	2.8
Prior Arrests	(%)
Possession of Marijuana	4.3
Alcohol Offense	4.3
Public Intoxication	2.1
Controlled Substance	1.4
Status	26.2
Public Disorder	17.7
Property	17.7
Resisting Law	5.0
Trespassing	6.4
Personal	14.9

[a] Many of the participants had multiple complaints for the same arrest (e.g., someone might have been picked up for both possession of marijuana and possession of paraphernalia). All charges were added together before computing the percentages for both current and prior complaints.

Other juveniles' parents called the police on them, because the child had come home smelling like alcohol or had gotten in a fight with them. It was clear that some of the parents did not, at the time, appreciate the gravity of turning their children over to the police for a drug offense. One mother told me she was very upset with the police because she had asked them to lock up her son for the night to "scare him straight," actually believing they would just let him go in the morning. The police arrested the youth, and the next day his mother was surprised when she received a call from the Juvenile Court informing her of her son's court date and listing the charges against him. School, however, served as the single largest source of drug busts.

Participants' Drug Use

Marijuana was by far the predominant drug of choice. Nevertheless, of those juveniles who used marijuana, only about half reported using it at the time they entered the JDC. About half reported using it only within the past year. The statistics in Table 3 reflect information only for those who reported having used the drugs in question. There were many who reported no alcohol use, for instance, who are not included in the frequency or last usage tables.[14]

The juveniles with whom I spoke gave various reasons for using marijuana. "It's a feeling of out of body-ness," one youth explained. "You're there, and then you're not there."

Relaxation was the most common reason given for smoking marijuana. As one youth put it, "It just relaxes you. You can be right all day."

"It just relieves stress," another said. "You don't have to worry."

Upon further reflection he added, "You do get paranoid. That's one thing."

"Why do you think that is?" I asked.

"Because it's illegal. You can get into big trouble like this, like where I'm at now."

The juveniles I spoke with reported that when they got high (before coming into the program, of course) they usually did the same things they did when they weren't high—talk with friends, eat, play, or listen to music, and such. "I do everything I do when I'm not high," reported one juvenile. "I'll play basketball. I kind of play a lot of sports. I'd go to school high. Actually, I did better when I was high."

Though most of them did not get high while at school, some of them felt it affected their studies anyway. A youth told me, "You feel like you're in another world. You don't feel like you have any problems. I don't have to think. You feel like you don't have any problems. You feel that there's nothing going on, which is some-times a bad thing. When you smoke it you feel like, 'I'm not worried.' "

"How can it be a bad thing?"

" 'Cause when you have school the next day, you say, 'I don't need to do my homework, man.' "

On the other hand, there were a few who had never used drugs more than once, but unfortunate circumstances had brought them into the court. In fact, several juveniles in the treatment program were assessed as not needing treatment. Some court staff attributed this to the local school district's program that, in part-nership with the police department, paid students $50 to turn in other students for possessing marijuana.

"That will often come when the kid receives an assessment," a staff member told me. "They'll be like, 'This kid does not need counseling.' With zero-tolerance that hurts those kids, because they're out of their education. The alternative schools are the bad of the bad kids. So you take a kid that was good, he just got set up or whatever, and you throw them into alternative school, and he's probably going to come out bad. I don't really agree with them there."

One juvenile, with whom I spoke, said he had found a bag of pot and told a neighbor he would give it to him. The neighbor called the cops on the youth, because the youth's friend had broken something of the neighbor's, and the neighbor wanted to get even. Before getting arrested, the juvenile said he had tried it once out of curiosity.

"It makes you cough," he told me.

"Did you get high?"

"I don't know. I didn't smoke very much."

I asked him if he felt he belonged in a drug treatment court.

"Yeah, I really do. I really do," he said. "I did try it once."

Meanwhile, another boy with whom I spoke claimed a rather active drug use history. "Well, I just smoked weed, because my body said that I needed it," he explained. "I've always had a tolerance to marijuana. I got the buzz you get, but nothin' like nobody else. That's why I did acid or Ecstasy or shrooms.

"[My drug of choice] was party drugs. That's like acid and Ecstasy—actually they call 'em club drugs—and shrooms. I did Ecstasy for the simple fact that it made me feel everything five times better. I could dance longer. It made sex better.

"Acid, it was a trip. Just sit there and just look at things and almost freak you out. Like, if I was on the drugs right now, I'd be seeing little green men jumping out of the walls at me. And shrooms just make you feel real good. See, I was manic depressive, and I did it before I was really diagnosed as it, and it made me feel real good."

He also smoked marijuana before school exams, " 'Cause it bailed me out, because I would have ate my pencils. I've already done that in the past, because I'm not a test taker. I freak out, especially when it's multiple choice. So I'll just start guessing and freaking out. I missed half of [an exam] two years ago because of that, because I kept freakin' out over it... [Marijuana] calmed me down, so I could actually read the questions.

"That's pretty much why I did it.... Calm me down. For like the first three periods [of school] I was great at paying attention and everything, but then afterwards, after it started goin' away, I was, you know, just like movin' around and shakin' and lookin' out the windows and not payin' attention, flunkin' class, 'til I finally got the idea that if I were to like find a way I could take this drug even without it being smelled, then I'd like that. So, that's when I started takin' Ecstasy... It lasted a whole lot longer."

The majority (65 percent) of primary diagnoses at referral were for cannabis abuse (see Table 3). Another 16 percent were diagnosed as "dependent." About a quarter of participants had a secondary diagnosis in their assessment as well. Alcohol abuse was the most common secondary diagnosis (though only for a few of the participants). For almost 90 percent of the participants, this program was their first time in drug treatment.

Just over 12 percent of the juveniles were diagnosed primarily with behavioral disorders. These included Attention Deficit Hyperactivity Disorder (ADHD) (characterized by "trouble paying attention," "trouble listening," "trouble finishing class work and homework," "interrupt[ing] or intrud[ing] on others" [American

Academy of Child and Adolescent Psychiatry, 2004a]) and Oppositional Defiance (characterized by "frequent temper tantrums,"
"excessive arguing with adults," "active defiance and refusal to
comply with adult requests and rules" [American Academy of
Child and Adolescent Psychiatry, 2004b]).

Table 3   **Participant Diagnoses**

Primary Diagnosis	(%)
Cannabis Abuse	65.9
Cannabis Dependence	16.3
Alcohol Abuse	3.9
Behavioral	12.4
Other	1.6

Secondary Diagnosis	(%)
Cannabis Abuse	3.4
Cannabis Dependence	0.6
Alcohol Abuse	13.0
Behavioral	6.2
Other	2.3
None	74.6

Received Treatment Before	12.2

Other times, the assessment stated simply "Behavioral Disorder" or "Disruptive Behavior." One youth who could not have
weighed over 100 pounds told me he was taking 80 mgs of Ritalin
a day, following a doctor's prescription when he came into the
program. The doctor changed the drug and reduced the amount
after a counselor complained that it was too much.

By far, anger problems dominated nondrug diagnoses. One
juvenile told me he attended night school because of his "anger
control problems." For some of these youths, marijuana use represented an attempt at self-medication. As a youth in the
program put it, "If I had never smoked marijuana, I'd probably be
in here for domestic violence or something else like that... murder
or something."

"It makes me relax," another youth explained. " 'Cause I have
a bad temper, like if somebody just looks at me crazy or gives me a
weird look... "

"Let me know if I do that."

"I just want to go hit them or something, and when I smoke weed it just calms me down. It's just like I don't care."

One of the counselors noted this problem with anger for some of the participants. "The question I usually ask them," the counselor said, "is, 'What reaction do you have if somebody does you wrong?' And every single time, so far every single time [they say], 'I'll get them back.'"

"And I'll say, 'Like do you use fistfights?' And usually they'll say something a lot worse like breaking out the windows, which one guy had actually done. Just recently I had a guy say he pulled out a gun on a boy... He said it wasn't loaded."

"They don't put two and two together. They don't think about the consequences. So I try to say, 'Think first... When I was growing up it was good old-fashion fistfights. I'm not telling you to do that, but if it comes to that, that would be a lot better than pulling out a gun. You surely won't get in as much trouble.'"

"And it's a culture of addiction and every aspect of that, and I'm trying to get them out of that. Because if they don't, they'll just keep getting worse, and I try to tell them every step they take farther and farther they get into it. And they're getting into it really right now."

Just over 40 percent of the first 177 participants had graduated by the end of the first year (see Table 4). It took graduates an average of seven months to complete the program. Those unsuccessfully terminated from the JDC were in for an average of 14 weeks before termination.

About a third of the participants had been expelled from the program. Almost 40 percent of the expelled participants were terminated because of a new charge. Another third were expelled for "noncompliance." Noncompliance generally consisted of habitually missing treatment meetings and/or disobeying parents (e.g., repeatedly violating curfew). Less than a quarter had been expelled for continued drug use or both continued drug use and noncompliance.

Consistent with drug courts' recognition of "relapse" as part of treatment, juveniles in the JDC must test positive for drugs more than once to be expelled for drug use only. Generally, the first couple of positive tests resulted in more intensive outpatient treatment schedules. Participants were often expelled after the third.

Table 4	Participant Outcomes	
Status	(%)	
Active:		
Phase 1	9.6	(17)
Phase 2	18.6	(33)
Completed	41.8	(74)
Expelled	29.9	(53)
Reason Expelled	(%)	
New Charge	39.5	
Noncompliance	31.6	
Continued Drug Use	7.9	
Drug Use and Noncompliance	15.8	
Other	5.3	
Weeks to Graduation	28.7 (mean)	
	28.3 (median)	
Weeks to Termination	14.6 (mean)	
	13.4 (median)	

I conducted this study while fulfilling a one-year contract as an evaluator for the JDC. Over the course of the year, I attended dozens of weekly compliance hearings in court, the prehearing staff meetings beforehand, and a few treatment meetings. During these observations, I chatted with staff and recorded notes. I interviewed 25 juveniles, the judge, defender, prosecutor, 3 probation officers, and 6 treatment counselors—37 people in all. A more detailed discussion of the methods and sample is presented in the appendix. In the following chapters, I share my observations, concerns, and hopes for the future that I came to hold while working in the JDC.

3 | DENIAL

With the kids, their denial is that they feel invincible, because they're kids.

JDC Counselor

They make you want to believe that you've got a problem. I may have a problem in finding direction, but I ain't got no drug problem.

JDC Juvenile

Client motivation for treatment has long been recognized by treatment professionals as one of the most important factors influencing therapy outcome.[15] In fact, it is often viewed as the fundamental prerequisite for treatment success (W. R. Miller, 1985). Research suggests, however, that clients in drug treatment often underestimate their need for treatment or help at admission or may even "deny that they have a problem or that they need to change their behavior or attitude" (Friedman, Granick, & Kreisher, 1994, p. 70). This lack of motivation in treatment is often attributed to personality traits, resistance, or overuse of defense mechanisms such as "denial" (W. R. Miller, 1985).

Robert White (1998) provides a comprehensive definition of denial:

> ...a psychological process that serves to keep the chemically dependent person out of touch with reality. It is one of the most difficult aspects of treatment for alcoholism and drug dependence. Denial is caused by numerous factors which act synergistically, including distortions of memory such as blackouts and euphoric recall, psychological defense mechanisms such as repression and projection, and social factors such as enabling by family and friends. It is common for chemically dependent people to ge-

nuinely believe that they do not have a problem with alcohol or other drugs in the face of overwhelming evidence to the contrary. (p. 9)

Much of the structure of drug courts, therefore, is designed to counteract the perceived threat of denial and other related defense mechanisms, which traditional adjudication may exacerbate. According to drug court proponents, the adversarial nature of the traditional criminal justice system can be a potential enabler of an offender's drug problem. The practices of traditional defense counsel and court procedures that encourage a defendant to deny guilt, it is argued, often reinforce the offender's denial of a drug problem (National Association of Drug Court Professionals, 1997).

Consequently, drug courts replace the adversarial model of justice with a collaborative model. The judge presides over the proceedings and makes decisions in collaboration with the defense and prosecution, who work together to keep the client compliant with the program requirements (USGAO, 1997). Depending on the jurisdiction, other social service and community organizations, such as probation and treatment providers, also collaborate with the court to enmesh the offender in a net of intervention.

For American juvenile courts, nonadversarial court proceedings are not new. As it was envisioned by nineteenth-century Progressives, the juvenile court system was meant to be an informal process where dispositions reflected the best interests of the child (Feld, 1993). The turn-of-the-century juvenile court movement had an antilegal slant, discouraging procedural formality and encouraging dependency on extra-legal resources (Platt, 1977). Because the juvenile court was seen as "benign, nonpunitive, and therapeutic," constitutional safeguards were not deemed necessary or appropriate (Feld, 1993, p. 203). Based on the legal doctrine of *parens patriae*, the state as parent, punishment was not seen as punitive but rather educational. It was meant to teach juveniles right from wrong. Defense attorneys in juvenile courts, therefore, have traditionally seen it as part of their duty, not just as public officials but also as adults, to impress their juvenile clients with the importance of telling the truth and to deter them from committing deviant acts in the future (Platt, 1977).

Under this paternalist approach to delinquency, juveniles were considered relatively helpless subjects in need of care and attention from the state and other professionals. Juvenile clients were often regarded by their lawyers as "subordinates and 'non-persons' who have little competence to appreciate their own behavior or determine where their best interests lie" (Platt, 1977, p. 175; Ainsworth, 1991).

In the 1960s and 1970s, this judicial paradigm came under increased scrutiny from critics on both sides of the political spectrum. Conservatives criticized the proceedings for being too permissive and encouraging disrespect for the law, while liberals argued that informal hearings allowed the court to inflict punishment without regard to due process or individual rights (Platt, 1977).

In 1967, the Supreme Court's *In re Gault* (387 U.S. 1) decision began the transformation of the juvenile court from the informal *parens patriae* model to a more formal scaled down version of adult criminal court (Ainsworth, 1991; Feld, 1993). The *Gault* decision identified two important disjunctions between juvenile justice rhetoric and its reality: (1) juvenile courts afforded very few procedural safeguards compared to adult courts and (2) the theory of benign rehabilitation was often at odds with the punitive reality of it. The Court decided that in practice the informal procedures resulted in broad and arbitrary discretion rather than the compassionate treatment sought by the proponents of the juvenile court (Ainsworth, 1991). Research on treatment programs had, meanwhile, been raising serious doubts about the effectiveness of coerced rehabilitation (Martinson, 1974; Feld, 1993).

Other court decisions followed, which brought the juvenile court procedure closer to that of adult courts. Jury trials are now often required. Guilt must be established beyond a reasonable doubt rather than by lower civil standards previously relied on. Nevertheless, some aspects of *parens patriae* can still be found in the juvenile courts (Ainsworth, 1991).

The drug court movement has revived many of the old themes associated with the Progressive Movement toward the rehabilitative ideal. Benign paternalism has reemerged to help drug addicts, seen as suffering from a disease that has eroded their own rational decision-making abilities. Just as their age makes children incapable of decisions regarding their own well-being, for proponents of drug courts, drug abusers now require the stewardship of the court system for "the best life outcome, not simply the best legal result" (*Cutting Crime*, quoted in Hora et al., 1999, p. 469).

According to this view, the adversarial model in the tradition-al paradigm enables drug users by encouraging them to deny guilt. Only through the benevolent collaboration between the court and treatment professionals can their "disease" be cured. Informal procedures, which encourage defendants to admit their guilt and addiction, are needed to overcome denial, one of the most difficult aspects of treatment for drug dependence.

The JDC

In the JDC, as in other drug courts, the prosecutor and defender work together as a team with the judge, treatment personnel, and probation and social service professionals in the community to help the offender deal with his or her drug use "or suffer the conse-quences" (National Association of Drug Court Professionals and The Office of Community Oriented Policing Services, 1998).

The JDC prosecutor explained, "We work together for the best solution for the child, and sometimes doing the mean thing or recommending two weeks in detention is not what is right for the child. And so we look at that... My big thing is accountability, where there has to be a consequence for an action. I tend to more consequences, where [the defender] also has to look at 'What does the child want? What can I get for him?'"

The public defender, too, must play a new role. "Under the traditional public defender's... role, you're there more to defend and preserve a kid's legal rights. In this program, it's a little bit different because it's kind of a diversion program... Therefore, the legal defending and the rights and things like that kind of don't apply. Because the purpose of this program is to get the kids... to be honest and admit anything that they've done.

"And then they get sanctioned and then they get rewarded and then at the end of the program they're going to get their charges dismissed. A traditional public defender... really [doesn't] have those options. It's just, you're going to defend your client, because either they're going to admit guilt, or you're going to defend them and say they're not guilty."

This can be a difficult transition for some defense attorneys who may worry that participants give up too many due process rights in order to gain entrance into the program. But proponents say that such reluctance stems from a misunderstanding of drug courts (Hora et al., 1999). Collaboration is better, because each team member is working in the best interest of the client. There are no adversaries working *against* the interests of the client. A better understanding of the collaborative nature of the drug courts, therefore, should "erode or completely extinguish the defense attorney's fear of leaving her client without legal protection from the state" (Hora et al., 1999, p. 521).

At the JDC, the defender did struggle at first with some aspects of the program initially.

"In the beginning, we had some problems that [the public defender] was not being a team player," a member of the staff said. "[The defender] was being a typical public defender. [The defender] was fighting for the client. That caused some friction. But really, I think [the defender] talked to [the defender's boss], and [the boss] explained a little more of the drug treatment program, and so now it's really good."

The defender agreed, "It was a hard transition for me... You just keep trying. There [were] a lot of days where I could get very angry, very upset... from some of the decisions and the things that would happen with the kids. But after you do something for a while... if you don't quit, you get tough skin... I just had to look at it as, what does the program set out to do? And if I were to do my traditional public defender job, the kids wouldn't learn anything. I would only facilitate the behavior that they had before they came into the program."

According to the court staff, in the interest of encouraging honesty among the participants, the JDC juveniles agree to give up certain protections against self-incrimination and other rights related to questioning. This can lead to far more aggressive questioning of juveniles thought to be lying about their drug use than one might see in a traditional juvenile court.

It was explained that "typically in a traditional setting, if the prosecutor's saying things that go against the rules of evidence, [the defender] objects. In this system, we really don't do that, because they're signing a plea agreement saying they're going to tell what happened."

While in the courtroom, I saw cases where juveniles would not admit to use despite one or more positive drug tests or other evidence, such as a fellow participant's testimony. Refusals to admit guilt would often result in rather tense questioning by the court staff. They were understandably incredulous of denials, and the uncooperative juveniles were told they were being disrespect-ful. Sometimes, levels of anger among the court staff would rise quite high.

If the denials persisted, the juveniles would sometimes receive extra punishment. One juvenile, for example, was assigned an essay on perjury, because, according to the court, his refusal to admit guilt would have been perjury in a regular court of law—a dubious legal claim, since in a "regular" court defendants cannot be forced to testify against themselves, but one that justified extra sanctions nonetheless. Detention was sometimes recommended by the prosecutor, but usually the judge just took that sanction "under advisement."

A JDC court team member explained the process: "Typically, in the very beginning, if you've been honest and you admitted the violation and there's no alleged perjury, it's community service [as punishment for the violation]. However, there are some kids who, at one of the hearings, [the court] might say, 'When was the last time you smoked marijuana?' and they may say, 'Well, umm.' It's like they get caught off guard, and of course they're not going to tell on themselves at that point. They'll say, 'Oh, when I got arrested.' Then we get that drug test back, and then it's positive, and then they admit that.

"So, a lot of times the judge will put them in detention for a night just on the basis of the perjury. Trying to teach the kids, 'Look, you don't need to lie. You've got to tell the truth.' But most of the time it's just community service."

Attempts at rationalizing or explaining an infraction could also lead to stiffer sanctions for a juvenile. On a holiday night, one juvenile with whom I spoke had violated her curfew and drank alcohol. She had not tested positive for any drugs during her tenure in the program prior to that, but her parents complained that curfew was becoming more of a problem.

The juvenile explained to the court that it was a holiday. "I thought, why not for one night?" She received 15 hours of commu-nity service, was moved up another level of Intensive Outpatient—treatment meetings two nights a week—and put on informal home detention. The prosecutor requested a night in detention, which was taken under advisement.

Some of the court staffers were later upset that the juvenile was not also put in detention, because she showed no remorse. The youth "did not realize it was wrong" and did not apologize, one court staffer complained. Instead, the juvenile explained the behavior as a holiday-induced lapse. Failing to show remorse for a violation could bring on worse punishments than the violation itself.[16]

Denial and Disagreement in Treatment

The issue of denial really came to the forefront in treatment. The JDC participants, having entered treatment because of an arrest rather than a fully voluntary decision to enter treatment independent of the judicial system were, for the most part, a reluctant treatment population. Many of the youth were clearly more concerned with the legal consequences of their use than with the use itself. In fact, legal factors were the driving force behind participation in the JDC. In my discussions with the juveniles, most mentioned getting their charges dropped as the biggest benefit to be gained by the program. Even those who said they were there primarily to give up drugs acknowledged that getting their charges dropped was certainly an inducement to participate.

Ambivalent about their drug use, some of the juveniles tended to be somewhat resistant in treatment meetings and reluctant to accept everything the counselors told them about their drug use. Often, this resistance was interpreted by the counselors as denial. The counselors attributed the juveniles' denial or resistance to their young age.

"With the kids, their denial is that they feel invincible because they're kids," a counselor told me. "They feel like 'Okay, if it happened to my buddy, big thing, because he probably wasn't smart enough.' Or you know, 'That was his luck, but if I put more time in it, more thinking in it, I won't have to turn out that way.' So they just really feel invincible.

"But again," she added, "I think with the kids we have to realize, too, that they just don't have the resources yet... They don't have the problem-solving skills. There are just different things that they haven't been able to tap into, so that keeps their denial pretty secure. But the more they can see there are other things that they can do, then that in itself, to me, kind of eats away at the denial, I think."

When I asked another counselor how much of a problem denial was for the juveniles, she replied, "Huge. They're very, very young.

They're at a stage of development that we all have been through where 'Nothing can hurt me. Nothing can touch me. I'm invincible.' And that's where they are. So it's a very, very difficult thing to convince or help a juvenile see their behavior has long-term consequences, because it's all about now."

As the counselors used the term, denial seemed to take on broader meaning, and its genesis lay not necessarily in the disease aspect of addiction, but in youth itself. Denial was treated less as a literal psychological condition symptomatic of chemical dependence and more as a general characteristic of youthfulness. *These kids are in denial simply because that's how kids are.*

Only one counselor did not feel denial was much of a problem with the juveniles. This assessment was based on drug use patterns, rather than the age of the youths. "I would say [denial] is probably more of a problem with adults than with the youth," she said. "I think that adults have had more years of experience with their drug of choice, and their denial systems are more solidly in place. With the kids, I don't know. I think because they're younger, because they don't have as much experience as some of the adults, if they do have a problem, they're going to admit it."

In the literature, denial is seen primarily as a coping mechanism of addicts, but only 17 percent of the JDC juveniles were diagnosed as dependent on any drug (mostly marijuana). The counselors, all of whom either were recovering addicts themselves or had someone close to them who was, however, insisted it was only a matter of time before the juveniles became dependent, too.

A counselor explained, "What I do is I try to let them know what options they have because most of them don't even think they have a problem. And some of them might not. They might just, you know…"

He stopped briefly, then started up again, reflecting, "because I can put myself in their shoes, and I remember the way it was when I was their age. The only problem is I didn't stop. I kept on going, and I try to tell them that. I try to tell them the consequences and inform them about what it's going to do to their bodies. Because they have been misinformed a lot of the time."

Most of the counselors avoided calling the juveniles addicts. For practical reasons alone, it was just not very useful in the treatment meetings. "I won't label them as being an addict," the same counselor said, "I just leave it as abuse, because I tell them,

'I never will label any of you anything.'" He said he could take the Diagnostic and Statistical Manual of Mental Disorders (DSM) into a meeting and go over criteria for addiction with each juvenile and say "you've hit this, this, and this. And I could say, 'I am calling you a drug addict.' But I don't try to do that. What good is that going to do?"

Given the juveniles' ambivalence toward their own drug use, it is not surprising that some of them felt there was a little too much "finger pointing," as a juvenile put it, by program staff. One youth summed it up, "I don't really like the [treatment] classes, because they make you think that you've got a problem, saying you're in denial."

Another complained that her counselor did not believe her when she told her how much alcohol and pot she had used. The youth said she rarely drank alcohol and she smoked marijuana on occasion. Either the counselor did not believe her or did not accept the notion of "occasional" use for juveniles.

"She thinks I used to do it all the time," the girl said of her counselor.

"She didn't believe you when you told how much you actually used?"

"Huh-uh," she shook her head. "I'm having the worst time of my whole life doing it and all that stuff."

Likewise, another juvenile complained about a treatment meeting in which he had told the counselor he drank alcohol once every couple of months. The counselor asked if he had ever experienced any problems when he drank, and he said, yes, he had suffered a hangover. He said the counselor told him he was an alcoholic. "Because I had a problem from the time I drank and I continued to drink later on, whether it's too much, then by definition I was an alcoholic," he explained to me. "When I said no, I wasn't an alcoholic, she'd say that I was in denial."

I just had some conflicts, because I knew alcohol wasn't something that I was dependent on. It wasn't something that I felt that I needed to do. It's like "Oh well, I'm at a fun party. What the heck." It's just a typical high school thing. Kids go to parties, and they drink. It doesn't mean that every kid that drinks and ends up with a hangover is an alcoholic."[17]

Although originally conceptualized as a coping mechanism for chemically dependent drug addicts, denial's meaning was broadening in the JDC to characterize youthfulness, then to encompass resistance to counselors' views. The juveniles' ambivalence toward their drug use and the conflict with counselors' definitions of that use became evidence of denial. Since the juveniles had not been diagnosed as dependent on drugs, the cause for this resistance-as-denial, instead, tended to be identified in the kids' young age and the feelings of invincibility that accompany youth.

Differing Definitions of Drug Abuse

The characterization of an individual in denial is ultimately left to the judgment of professionals or others in authority. In light of the difficulty researchers have had in actually discovering an objectively identifiable denial trait, such judgments might sometimes be based heavily on these authorities' subjective perceptions (W. R. Miller, 1985). These perceptions of denial often reflect the extent to which the client accepts the authority's definitions of the issues.

Denial in the JDC seemed most often the product of the juveniles' refusal to accept staff's definitions of drug abuse. Indeed, definitions of drug abuse and drug problems presented a clear split between staff and youth. Many youths, and sometimes their parents, believed that moderate use of alcohol and marijuana was at least possible, while staff tended to view any use as abuse, several believing any use was a likely gateway to addiction. Though staff and juveniles also differed somewhat among themselves, the overall consistency of the two groups' points of view is noteworthy. When asked if they felt they had a drug problem, most of the juveniles said no.

"Me? Honestly, I don't think I do," responded one juvenile, "but a lot of people say that if you're in denial, then that's the first step. So, right now I'm really uncertain. They said to be addicted you smoke every day. I never really smoked it every day or anything."

"How would you define a drug problem?"

"A drug problem... to me it's not smoking every day, it's just a want or need for it all of the time."

Some of the juveniles did report they had a problem, and one youth really embraced the drug use as disease model. "There is no such thing as using responsibly," he told me. "Nobody can use responsibly? People can't drink responsibly?"

"Nope, because you think you are, but you're not because once you say you drink responsibly, you're an alcoholic because you can't stop having even a drink. 'Cause if you have just this much," he pinched his index finger and thumb together indicating a tiny amount, "then you'll get more."

"Is that true for everybody?"

"It's true. It's a proven fact. Statistics say it is."

This boy notwithstanding, the differing notions of moderate or responsible drug use between the youths and the JDC staff, seemed to lie at the foundation of the conflict over denial and addiction. The staff rejected most notions of responsible use, especially for marijuana and other illicit drugs. (One staff member also felt that alcohol could not be used responsibly by anyone, juvenile or adult.) And the staff members were reluctant to acknowledge the possibility of moderate use. For them, all use was abuse. The juveniles, on the other hand, almost invariably distinguished between moderate use and abuse. When staff did acknowledge the possibility of responsible use, they emphasized the importance of the legal status of the drug and the age of the user as prerequisites for responsibility.

"Because I don't think kids have good enough judgment yet," a court member explained, "not that many adults have good judgment—that's kind of a ridiculous statement—but I think kids have a hard enough time dealing with issues of peer pressure and boundaries, more so than adults. If you then put in a mood altering or an inhibition releasing substance, you're going to have some problems. I guess it just makes it more of a challenge for kids to behave responsibly... it just kind of stacks the deck."

Perhaps not surprisingly, no juvenile mentioned age as a variable influencing responsibility. They tended to define responsible use versus irresponsible use in terms of quantity used and whether the person "needed" the drug. In applying these rules, they did not report age as a factor, nor did they distinguish between alcohol and marijuana, or legal and illegal drugs. Most drugs could be used responsibly so long as the use was moderate and the person did not "need" it.

As a youth explained, "There are a few of my friends who I honestly think are responsible. It's just a rare occasion type of thing. There are kids at my school who will go out every day after school and smoke marijuana, and there are kids who might smoke twice a month or drink twice a month. I find that, even though it is illegal, I do think it is responsible. As far as alcohol goes, the legal age is 21, but I think a 16-year-old can drink more responsibly than a 21-year-old as long as they don't let it get carried away."

Just about the whole staff distinguished between legal and illegal drugs, however, believing that illegal drugs, by their very illegality, could not be used responsibly. A court member explained, "Whether or not you're breaking the law is part of acting responsibly, because I think that if you start down the road of saying, 'It's okay to break this law or that law,' then suddenly you don't learn any sort of structure or values and any respect for it."

Of course, most of the juveniles, having been arrested and put into the drug court treatment program, and some kicked out of school, recognized the link between drug laws and problems with drugs. They just put a different spin on it.

"I mean, drugs can always give you a problem," one of the juveniles told me. "You can smoke weed for the first time, and it won't make you stupid right away. But you can get arrested, and that's a problem. So, I don't think... Yes, I had a drug problem, but I wasn't addicted... My drug problem was I would smoke marijuana in stupid places where I could get caught."

Indeed, for many of the juveniles, a drug problem was more a question of getting caught and the resulting consequences. Several youths told me that the most important lesson they learned in the JDC was to leave their marijuana at home. "I'll know next time, and I won't have it on me," a juvenile said. "If you catch a case with marijuana, you have to go through too much."

Another affirmed, "I won't have it on me next time. I'll be smarter."

One counselor acknowledged this distinction between law-related drug problems and other types. "I don't think they all do [have a drug problem]. I think they've all had a problem *with* drugs, because, I mean, they got caught doing something they weren't supposed to be doing. But I think most of them are at a place where this early intervention can really make a difference."

Tensions grew in the court and in treatment when juveniles suggested that many of their problems were evidence of bad drug laws more than irresponsible drug abuse. A counselor explained this conflict to me: "Most of the people that drink a few beers drink it because it gives them a little bit of a buzz, but that's all. So if that is what society calls social drinking, okay, I can live with that. But the kids can argue right back, 'Well if you smoke a joint, one joint at home, what does that hurt?' I can't really argue that, and it's a tough one to argue, and I can't argue, and I don't even try. That's when I go right back to 'I will talk to you [when pot] is legalized,' and they hate it. They hate it."

The movement to reform marijuana laws, when thrown into the mix, also presented a problem for the counselors. Though I never brought it up, the debate over legalizing marijuana was an occasionally recurring topic in my interviews. When I asked one court staff member whether she felt marijuana could be used responsibly, for instance, she mused, rephrasing the question back to me, "Should marijuana be legal?"

Several of the juveniles also volunteered that they felt marijuana should be legalized.

"It's not like marijuana is like cocaine," explained one youth. "You don't have to send me to a rehab place. Marijuana is not crack. You don't have to send me to rehab... So it's ridiculous that weed is illegal. The government would make a lot more money if they just taxed it, instead of spending money on trying to make a war against it."

The youth were reluctant to accept the definition of drug abuse as all illicit drug use, and many of them brought this up during the treatment meetings, particularly when they compared marijuana to alcohol. A counselor said that the kids know marijuana does not have the withdrawal effects seen with alcohol, "and so they call me on that, and they say, 'Well, you know alcohol is legal and look what it does.' And I don't have any argument."

One time before court, a juvenile's mother told a JDC staff member that she knows "a lot of doctors and lawyers who smoke pot." To this the staffer responded matter-of-factly, "That's fine, but it's still illegal."

Indeed, according to one counselor, the juveniles were not the only ones in denial. "The parents are in a lot of denial," a counselor explained. "The parents—and I want to be fair to the parents—some of them are just burnt out. Some of them are single parents. They're working a lot of hours. So, Johnny's gotten in trouble once before, and they worked through that, and now he got in trouble again, and got in trouble again, so they're feeling overwhelmed... You know, a lot of them are angry at the fact that they do have to go through this with their child."

Differences over definitions of drug abuse and drug use, and the conflict those differences engender, are hardly unique to the JDC. Professionals also have different points of view on drug use and abuse. In its broadest and most legalistic sense, drug abuse has been defined as any use of a prohibited drug or the use of a medical drug in a manner deviating from approved medical patterns. The ONDCP (2002), for instance, makes no distinction between use and abuse of prohibited drugs. All use is abuse. Likewise, the United Nations (1992) "discourages the use of all of the following terms and concepts: 'recreational use' of drugs, 'responsible use' of drugs, 'decriminalization,' and defining drugs as 'hard' or 'soft.'"

A survey of substance abuse experts produced a definition of drug abuse as "any use of drugs that causes physical, psychological, economic, legal, or social harm to the individual user or to others affected by the drug user's behavior" (Rinaldi, Steindler, Wilford, & Goodwin, 1988, p. 557). By this definition, all of the juveniles were drug abusers, because their arrest clearly indicated legal trouble resulting from their drug use.

In British drug courts, not all illicit drug use is considered abusive (Nolan, 2002). A chief probation officer involved in drug courts in England, for example, identified several gradations of drug use, such as experimental use, recreational use, problematic use, and dependent use. "People use drugs in the main because they enjoy it," he said. "And the vast majority of people in our society or [in America] use drugs in a non-problematic way" (quoted in Nolan, 2002, p. 96).

Some observers note that definitions of bad or excessive use are, like denial, often a matter of who is defining the use (De Rios & Smith, 1977, p. 18). Drug abuse, according to Duncan (1992), is "an interactional process among the drug, the drug-taker, and the circumstances of the drug-taking: drug, set, and setting" (p. 319). It is a function of the interaction between an individual and his or her environment. In the words of the JDC youth, "My drug problem was I would smoke marijuana in stupid places where I could get caught."

Increasingly, drug abuse has become a shorthand term to differentiate licit and illicit drug use, instead of referring to an actual typology of drug using behaviors (Drug Abuse Council, 1980; cited in Duncan, 1992, p. 317). Substituting legal status for actual health or behavioral criteria in the definition of drug abuse prevents us from understanding drug abuse. Peele and Brodsky (2001) suggest that the first step in drug policy should be to "acknowledge the difference between exposure to drugs and drug abuse" (p. 62). Acknowledging potentially healthy relationships with drugs allows us to better identify unhealthy ones. "This may sound heretical to the professionals who readily categorize all illicit drug use as abuse. But the refusal to recognize healthy relationships with stigmatized drugs hinders our understanding of drug-related problems and healthy relationships with them" (Whiteacre & Pepinsky, 2002, p. 27).

According to Duncan (1992), "It is simply not realistic to say that all use of any particular drug, however socially disapproved it may be, is necessarily abuse" (p. 318). Duncan warns that relying on such "pat answers" to these difficult questions will only do more harm than good.

Legal definitions of drug abuse, moreover, become circular. For the JDC staff, juveniles are in the drug court, because they are drug abusers. They know the youths are drug abusers, because they have been arrested and put into the drug court. In this way drug abuse becomes intertwined with the law and legal authority. The more one violates legal authority and the legal structure, the more of a drug abuser one is. To disagree with this is to be in denial, thus further demonstrating one's drug abuse problem. Discussion becomes impossible. Other points of view are ruled out by self-evident circularity.

As such, what was once a therapeutic tool becomes, in practice, a tool for maintaining legal authority and the authority of the drug court. Disagreement with program staff becomes a symptom of a disease in need of treatment. Thus, denial of a drug problem risks becoming a denial of the legitimacy of the program itself, whose sole purpose is to treat and cure addicts and abusers. The youths' insistence that they do not want or need treatment undermines the court's role as parent, leaving only the sheen of state power. Therapeutic discourse becomes a means of reasserting that power for the client's best interests.

Allen (1981) argues, "A successful rehabilitative program requires the perception of its legitimacy, both in the public that authorizes it and also in the subjects of the program. Among both groups, and particularly in the second, this sense of legitimacy has weakened" (p. 30). Indeed, Nolan (2001) claims that the drug court movement represents an effort to remedy the court system's perceived deficit of legitimation in the eyes of the public. He quotes a judge speaking before a large group of drug court professionals, who warned, "If we don't change what we are doing in the next few years, and if we don't change how we go about serving the community with more relevancy, with more meaning, we are going to find that in twenty-five years, we have become irrelevant in the minds of the public" (p. 58).

Perhaps, the JDC compliance hearings provide an opportunity for those involved to come together and, through the assessment of participant compliance, reaffirm the court and its potential to help those who want it. Often the judge would congratulate a compliant juvenile with a statement emphasizing the program's role in helping the child. "You've been testing negative, so the counseling must be working. You must be learning." Or "The proof is in the pudding. You obviously are learning something," with which the juvenile would verbally agree.

Although quite a few juveniles complained to me that the required eight-hour drug education class was boring and that they learned little if anything, I never heard one respond, "No, I learned very little, and my mom really hated sitting through the drug education class."

The reaffirmations of the compliance hearings provide a certain degree of program legitimation for all in the court to witness. The stories of program support through individual success and struggle make up much of the "therapeutic theater" of the drug treatment court (Nolan, 2001). This is important for drug courts, which were a response to a crisis brought about by the criminal justice system itself in its punitive war on drugs. It is particularly important for a program under the close scrutiny of probation and the traditional court system that sometimes views the diversionary program as, to quote one court program staff member, "a Mickey Mouse court." As the next chapters on punishment and surveillance show, it is no Disneyland (well, maybe the surveillance is close).

4 | SANCTIONS IN TREATMENT

There's been a lot of kinks as to the focus...you know, whether it's more treatment based or whether it's more punishment based.

JDC Staff Member

This is a pretty good program. It's not overly punitive, and it doesn't really let me off too easily for the mistakes I made.

JDC Juvenile

Like other drug courts, the JDC relies on a system of graduated punishments and rewards to encourage participants' compliance and hold them accountable for their actions.[18] Noncompliance is punished through verbal admonition by the judge, community service, essay writing, compulsory attendance at more compliance hearings, a more intensive treatment schedule, additional drug tests, informal home detention (the juvenile may not leave home unless accompanied by a parent), formal home detention (the juvenile may not leave home or have friends over), short-term incarceration, and ultimately termination from the program followed by criminal proceedings. Compliant participants receive rewards such as verbal praise from the judge and other court members, gift certificates for movies or restaurants, and long intervals between compliance hearings. Upon successful completion of the program, the juvenile's charges are dismissed and record expunged.

For proponents, sanctions hold offenders accountable for their behaviors, and if used properly, they do not simply punish undesirable behavior but "augment the treatment process" as well (USGAO, cited in Hora et al., 1999, p. 469). The sanctioning system is meant to help shape offenders' behavior by encouraging healthy behavior and discouraging drug use and rule violations (Marlowe & Kirby, 1999).

This approach moves beyond the "traditional clinical wisdom," which holds that coercing treatment is counterproductive (Marlowe & Kirby, 1999). For proponents of drug courts, punishment and therapy are collaborative rather than contradictory goals. "The traditional dichotomy between these two does not and does not need to exist" (quoted in Nolan, 2001, p. 52).

In fact, when used as an adjunct to therapy, aversive sanctions are not even punishments in the usual sense. Rather, they are "smart punishments," which consist of "the imposition of the minimum amount of punishment necessary to achieve the twin sentencing goals of reduced criminality and drug usage" (Tauber, 1994, p. 9). And "smart punishment" is "not really punishment at all, but a therapeutic response to the realistic behavior of drug offenders in the grip of addiction" (Hora et al., 1999, p. 470).[19]

Punishment and treatment have become so intertwined that in its 2002 National Drug Control Strategy, the ONDCP called these elements of their drug control program "two sides of the same coin" (p. 4).

> Most drug users—the lucky ones, at least—are no strangers to coercion. People in need of drug treatment are fortunate if they run up against the compassionate coercion of family, friends, employers, the criminal justice system, and others. Such pressure needs no excuse; the health and safety of the addicted individual, as well as that of the community, require it. Compassionate coercion begins with family, friends, and the community. (ONDCP, 2002, p. 15)

Nolan (2001) attributes the astonishing growth of the drug court movement to this ideological compromise that promises to both rehabilitate and punish. Conservatives support its tough, intrusive nature, and liberals support its ostensibly more humanitarian and rehabilitative qualities (Nolan, 2001). It provides treatment without being "soft on crime."[20]

One could argue that coercive treatment is not a revolution in America's approach to drugs so much as a new twist on an old theme. Coercive treatment practices have existed within America's law enforcement approach to drug use, premised on control and punishment, since the Harrison Narcotics Act of 1914 (Farabee, Prendergast, & Anglin, 1998; Quinn, 2000).[21] In the 1930s, federal narcotics treatment farms were established in Fort Worth, Texas, and Lexington, Kentucky. Opiate users were often incarcerated in these facilities where they were treated for their addictions. In practice, these farms were nothing more than "glorified prisons" (Nolan, 2001, p. 32).

In the 1960s, broad-based civil commitment procedures for addicts were implemented in the federal system and in the New York and California state systems (Farabee et al., 1998). These civil commitment programs were short-lived and of doubtful efficacy (Nolan, 2001). The approach did, however, presage increased cooperation between the therapeutic and justice communities (Nolan, 2001).

By the mid-1970s, civil commitment programs were largely replaced by more community-based treatment centers (De Leon, 1988). In 1972, the federal government funded the first Treatment Alternatives to Street Crime (TASC) project in Wilmington, Delaware. Consistent with the shift toward punitive-based treatment, TASC now stands for Treatment Accountability for Safe Communities. Treatment is no longer seen as an alternative to regular punishment; it is now a tool for "accountability."

Providing a bridge between treatment institutions and the criminal justice system, TASC has utilized "innovative criminal dispositions" to motivate drug-using offenders to cooperate with treatment (BJS, 1992). These strategies could include diversion, pretrial intervention, probation, and other community sentencing. If granted diversion, offenders enter community-based treatment, and TASC monitors those participants for compliance with treatment. The TASC model is the predecessor of the modern drug treatment court, and in some drug courts, TASC programs serve case management and other services as contracted providers.

By 1998, the criminal justice system was responsible for 40-50 percent of referrals to community-based treatment programs (Farabee et al., 1998). This portion has continued to grow. In light of the nation's high proportion of criminal justice treatment clients, the therapeutic value of coercing offenders into treatment represents a major policy and program issue in drug treatment (Farabee et al., 1998). Program evaluations of mandatory drug treatment, which look at recidivism and drug use, however, present equivocal assessments of the value of coercion.

The Treatment Outcome Prospective Study (TOPS) was a large-scale study of treatment clients from 10 cities who entered over 40 publicly funded outpatient methadone, residential, and outpatient drug-free drug abuse programs from 1979 to 1981 (Hubbard, Collins, Rachal, & Cavanaugh, 1988). Several TASC programs were included in the study. During treatment, both voluntary and legally referred outpatient drug-free clients reported fewer symptoms of depression, less drug use, fewer criminal acts and increased levels of employment (Hubbard et al., 1988). There were no significant differences in posttreatment crime between legally referred and nonlegally referred treatment clients (Hubbard et al., 1988).

In 1998, Farabee and associates reviewed the findings of 11 studies on the use of coercion in drug treatment. Of the 11 studies, 5 found a positive relationship between criminal justice referral and treatment outcomes, 4 reported no difference, and 2 studies reported a negative relationship.

Roman and Harrell (2001) conducted a cost-benefit analysis of a graduated sanctioning drug court program for felony drug defendants. They compared defendants in the *sanctions docket*, which closely monitored and drug tested defendants and responded to program violations, "with swift and certain application of clearly defined penalties," with defendants in the *standard docket*, which offered drug testing and judicial monitoring but no enhanced treatment or graduated sanctions (Roman and Harrell, 2001, p. 242). They found that the sanctions program participants were significantly less likely to reoffend in the year following sentencing, measured by both official arrest records and a self-report survey. The researchers concluded that the graduated sanctions program yielded "a net benefit in reduced cost of crime of about two dollars for each dollar spent treating participants in the sanctions programs" (Roman and Harrell, 2001, p. 264).

Some methodological issues, however, mediate these results. Though initially defendants were randomly chosen for eligibility in the sanctions group or the standard group, defendants deemed eligible for the sanctions group were ultimately *invited* to participate in the program. Just over one-third (34 percent) of those eligible declined to participate, suggesting a significant level of selection bias. All those assigned to the standard docket, meanwhile, went through it.

In such circumstances, a self-selection process among the 64 percent of the experimental group who opted to participate in a program with extra punishments seems quite likely. Undoubtedly, they differed from others on motivation or other factors not measured in the research. This "skimming" of the experimental group through self-selection makes comparisons between the two groups problematic. Moreover, the two tracks differed on more variables than just the presence or absence of graduated sanctions. For example, there was no case management in place to assist standard docket participants in finding treatment if the judge encouraged it (Roman & Harrell, 2001, p. 243). Given these constraints, one cannot draw confident conclusions regarding the effects of court sanctions on drug treatment for defendants.

In another study of treatment participation, probationers had higher treatment attendance rates than voluntary admissions, but only 16 percent of probationers continued treatment after their probation period (Rosenberg & Liftik, 1976; Farabee et al., 1998). Evidence suggests that when treatment is coerced "compliance characteristically ends at its termination" (W. R. Miller, 1985). On the other hand, some researchers point out that any reduced recidivism, even if only during the treatment period, qualifies as a public good.

In the JDC, sanctions are present at the start. Though participation in the program is ostensibly voluntary, the juveniles and their parents make their decision under the combined forces of a recent arrest and the likelihood of being prosecuted and put on probation versus the possibility of having the charges dropped and their record expunged upon completion of the JDC program. A staff member explained,

> Actually, the kids don't have a choice. They have a choice, but... our intake unit screens the child for the drug court, and they tell the family that they're going to meet with the drug court [probation officer], and then they do. And once the families hear that the case can be dismissed, and it's really intense counseling, and the court pays for it, they're usually likely to go to drug court rather than regular probation... I think a big seller is that [charges get] dismissed. In regular probation it doesn't get dismissed, and then it's not expunged either. You have to petition the court to get it expunged.

Many of the juveniles readily admitted that their original motivation to enter the program was simply to get their charges dismissed. Several even said that getting their charges dropped was the only benefit they anticipated getting out of the program. Some also believed, incorrectly, that it would be easier than regular probation. A few, though, did not even realize that the program was voluntary; their parents had simply made the decision.

One punishment popular among some staff was the essay writing. A staff member explained, "If they're not going to think about anything else, at least if they have to sit down and write it down, at least they're going to think about it." The essays were generally one or two pages long, and the subject matter ranged from the dangers of drugs to apology letters to parents, "because your mom now is going to have to drive you to counseling twice a week," a staff member said. "She's going to have to spend more time in this program, and you have affected her."

Generally, the participants thus sanctioned said that they did not much mind writing the essays, and they felt they learned from the exercise. One juvenile did share her troubles she faced trying to write an essay on the dangers of marijuana use.

"It was hard," she said, " 'cause I was looking up stuff on the Internet about weed and why it's dangerous, 'cause that's what the essay was supposed to be about. I couldn't find anything on why it was bad. Everything was why it was good." Instead, she focused on the consequences of getting caught.

Community service was another common punishment for violations such as a positive drug test or missing a counseling meeting. A juvenile might be assigned 10-15 hours at a place like Goodwill or the Salvation Army. A staffer observed that "most of them don't like it, obviously. We've had some who said they liked it, and they're going to continue to do it. Who knows if that will be true."

One juvenile who was assigned to community service said it was "mind numbing." He spent the day arranging and folding clothes at a Goodwill store. "I really wouldn't even classify that as community service," he said. "When I think of community service, I think about helping people like disadvantaged youth or kids in poverty or whatever... If I'm going to do community service, I want to get something out of it."

A JDC staffer explained, "Of course, very few kids are going to be like... 'Please give me community service.' When they do, you know you've taught them something. There have been kids who have been like, [after completing] community service, 'I understand I did wrong.' When that happens, I am thrilled. It means they have learned that there's a consequence for what they did wrong. At least I hope that's what it means, and it's not like... 'Community service, that's so easy let me do it again.'"

Punishment and therapy are strange bedfellows in the drug court. The graduated sanctioning schedule is expected to be sufficiently aversive to encourage participant compliance with program rules. At the same time, the punishments are also meant to help rehabilitate. To serve its purpose for the JDC, community service must somehow be both uncomfortable enough to serve as a punishment and rewarding enough to represent rehabilitation. For the juveniles to want to do more community service means the court has "taught them something"—unless it means instead that it was not a sufficiently punitive sanction.

The ambiguity of community service as a punitive sanction is not unique to the JDC.[22] In the National Evaluation of Juvenile Drug Courts, researchers with the Urban Institute found that community service in one drug court served as either a punishment or a reward, depending on the child (Rossman et al., 2004). "Resistant youth" were sometimes assigned to assist the police in certain community services as a punishment, while other youth who enjoyed doing the activities received the assignments as rewards for compliance (Rossman et al., 2004).

Some recalcitrant youth in the JDC were held in the detention center overnight. Detention was reserved for juveniles who were perceived as dishonest (i.e., denied using a drug but tested positive) or who continued to violate program rules. Unfortunately, at the time I was there the staff did not keep a record of who was incarcerated in the detention facility as a sanction, the date of detention, or the length. The program coordinator began officially tracking this just before I left.

The juveniles with whom I spoke held divergent opinions on the punishments. One youth complained, "I don't know. It's like they ask you to do community service and all, and put you on home detention just for little bitty stuff."

"This is a pretty good program," said another. "It's not overly punitive, and it doesn't really let me off too easily for the mistakes I made."

On the other hand, he did feel that sometimes the JDC's sanctioning schedule was a little too rigid. "I haven't been late yet, but every now and then I see kids coming in [to a treatment meeting] like ten minutes late, and they have a good excuse, but they'll say, 'No, you're counted as absent for the whole time.'" An understandable gripe, considering the juveniles felt the court staff was consistently late getting the hearings started.

The drug court literature generally recommends the "carrot and stick" combination of both positive and negative sanctions, but each JDC staff member clearly had a preference for one or the other. Some favored rewards as more effective than punishments. One court member explained, "I know when I first started, they told me one of the tenets of the program is that at least [the juveniles] get positive reinforcement that they may not get at home... A lot of kids get excited when they hear 'You've done good.' Even though they're doing good, they like to hear it because we all do. I'd like it if I came to work, and my boss is like 'Hey, you did a great job yesterday.'"

Many of the juveniles did seem to appreciate the rewards. Some cited the movie tickets as the best thing about the court hearings. "It's nice to know that you're doing good every once in a while," one youth said.

Another observed glibly, "You don't have to do anything for [the rewards]. I get in trouble, and they give me things."

Some staff members questioned the efficacy of the rewards. "I think the sanctions might have more effect than a reward," a staff member said. "I don't see a lot of teens getting excited about McDonald's money or movie tickets."

Conflict sometimes arose between staff who felt there was too little punishment and those who felt there was plenty. A probation officer said, "There's been a lot of kinks as to the focus... You know, whether it's more treatment based or whether it's more punishment based. [A co-worker] and I are probation officers, so it's hard for us... We're trained to be punishment-based. This is what we do, and you have to do this and you have to do that or you're going to be violated, period. But it's a treatment court everyone says. You have to expect them to get a dirty rap [positive drug test]. You have to expect them to do this; or we'll give them a second, third, tenth chance before we violate them and sometimes [the probation officer] and I are like, 'Okay, what does it take to get rid of a kid?'"

Another probation officer explained, "When I make recommendations, I feel like I'm trying to punish them as much as they possibly could get punished for what they did. The judge has the ultimate decision, obviously, so sometimes we don't get our recommendations."

A treatment counselor shared much of the same sentiment, complaining that punishments did not seem swift or severe enough. "I've had kids in the JDC who've continued to use and have gotten no repercussions, whereas I would give repercussions. I would bump them up another group level. I might give them what's called a '90 in 90'... It's 90 meetings in 90 days. I might give them a special assignment to do, you know. I might ask them to seek a sponsor. And if they didn't choose to go with that, then I'd terminate their treatment and recommend that they go inpatient... I have kids that, you know, keep coming to me over and over again, and this is one of the problems that I see, and I don't know what [the court is] doing about it. Maybe there's something they're doing about it. I don't know."

Some of the court staff members, however, felt they had been a little too strict with punishments early in the program, monitoring the juveniles' every behavior, and the permissiveness perceived by the others had resulted from the court's efforts to step back a little. A court member recalled, "When we first started, we were kind of policing every little thing that they did. And then, you know, we had to kind of step back and say, 'Wait a minute. We can't be parents to these kids...' So if someone gets in a fight with their brother or sister, I don't think they should be detained or given community service. Maybe write an apology letter. But there were times in the beginning, that we were giving heavy sanctions for any type of negative behavior."

The literature on drug courts often glosses over the uncertainty, disagreement, and tensions that accompany the use of sanctioning strategies in a drug court. Former director of the National Drug Court Institute, Judge Tauber (1993), states "You don't have to be an expert in behavior modification to be an effective Drug Court Judge (although some basic knowledge of behavioral theory would be helpful). Rely on your common sense knowledge of what works in motivating people (i.e., as a parent, etc.)" (p. 9). The experiences in the JDC, however, suggest that in everyday practice "common sense knowledge of what works" is not always shared among all players.

This disagreement was most evident regarding the termination of noncompliant juveniles from the JDC program. A couple of the staff felt that the judge was too slow to terminate noncompliant juveniles.

"I would probably be more tough on the kids," said a staff member. "I think this is a great program, and this is an opportunity. You get the chance to get your case dismissed. Kids that tamper with their urine screens or test dirty after being clean for several months or have had several violations, they need to be expelled. I don't have the—I don't know if you want to call it patience—but I feel like this is an opportunity, and they're not taking advantage of it. So why should we continue to give it to them?"

The JDC is faced with the irony that its ultimate sanction (other than detention[23]), terminating a juvenile from the program, might actually be little punishment at all. Had they not entered the JDC, most of the juveniles would have been put on probation where they would see a probation officer less often, be randomly tested for drugs fewer times, and report back to court in 90 days. If the juvenile on probation complies with all of these requirements, he or she can be off probation in about the same time as the JDC juvenile with fewer court hearings, fewer drug tests, and often fewer treatment sessions, depending on the terms of probation. The JDC, however, dismisses the charges upon program completion, an important reward for compliance. It is interesting that some members of regular probation viewed the JDC as a "Mickey Mouse" court, even though many of the juveniles said they would have preferred regular probation, because it was easier.

"If [the judge] sees when they get expelled they're going to regular probation, [the judge] sees that as the easy way out," a staff member explained. "I think that's why [the judge] keeps them in. I'm not sure... I understand the idea that the easy way out is going to regular probation, but we've already offered him the resources; and 9 times out of 10 he's gone to as much counseling as possible, and he's still continuing to use and continuing to act out. There's another kid out there that needs the opportunity to succeed in the program."

Some of the juveniles in the program agreed it was difficult to get expelled. One youth said he wanted to get out of the JDC but couldn't seem to get out. Feeling that he did not have a drug problem and did not need the rigorous program, he was frustrated by the program. "I don't think I should be in this program," he said. "I think I should be on probation. I should definitely get punished because I did break the law." Shortly after the interview, he was finally terminated from the program.

Another juvenile who also eventually terminated from the program complained, "They have too much expectation in this program. They want you to do this and do that. On the other hand, it's alright, but I think I'd be better off on regular probation than this... They give you a lot of chances in this program, but I'd rather be in regular probation, [because] you go through it quicker, and then you don't have to get drug tests like this... It would have been better for me, and you go to court way more times in this program than you do in the other court."

The court does allow juveniles to quit the program, but staff members point out that probation requires drug tests and treatment, too. Only on probation, the court does not pay for it and one's arrest is not dismissed. Nevertheless, for some juveniles, the treatment requirements of the JDC were more than they were willing to do. Besides, a juvenile's records are sealed once the youth turns 18, effectively "erasing" one's charges anyway.

This situation is not unique to the JDC. Many proponents of drug courts emphasize that the program is often a more onerous alternative to traditional probation. "[Drug courts] generally obligate a defendant to make more frequent court appearances and force the defendant to undertake forms of treatment which place more burdens on the defendant than normal probation" (Hora et al., 1999, pp. 522–523). This point underscores the argument that drug courts are not "soft on crime," and is a crucial aspect of the rehabilitation/punishment compromise, leading to the widespread popularity of drug courts (Nolan, 2001).

Coercion, whether used by itself or in conjunction with therapeutic goals, has been the backbone of America's criminal justice approach to illicit drug use since the Harrison Narcotics Act of 1914. Drug courts represent one more chapter of this ongoing story. As such, proponents have accepted coerced treatment uncritically. Nevertheless, despite the drug court literature's tendency to present graduated sanctioning systems as "common sense" interventions that have successfully merged and negated traditional antagonisms between punishment and treatment, there still seems to be some considerable disagreement among staff.

The sanctioning system, set up in the JDC to be both therapeutic and punitive, is interpreted differently by its staff, the participants, and other criminal justice programs, but these ideas have yet to become the focus of discourse among researchers of drug courts. Tensions experienced by staff and juveniles influence the therapeutic tools of the JDC. As is discussed in the next chapter, staff, especially the counselors, also experience internal personal tensions about the use of coercion as a therapeutic tool.

5 | AMBIVALENCE AND ACCOUNTABILITY

There has to be consequences. There has to be consequences. It breaks my heart, but there's a line as far as being an enabler.

JDC Counselor

"Responsible" is like when you're told to do something and you actually do it.

JDC Juvenile

In 1953, C.S. Lewis wrote an essay in *Res Judicatae*, criticizing what he called the "Humanitarian Theory of Punishment," the notion that punishment should be intended only to "mend the criminal" or deter others from committing the offense.[24] The humanitarian theory of punishment assumes that deviance is a pathological condition, like a disease, in need of a cure, rather than a moral decision deserving retribution. Punishment, therefore, should be therapeutic instead of punitive or retributive, and as long as it is so, there is no reason to limit it. It is meant to help, not hurt.

Lewis argued, however, that punishments, irrespective of the rationale behind them or the labels given them, are still experienced as punitive.[25] Besides, according to Lewis, crime is a moral problem, and a criminal should be punished simply because he deserves to be. By keeping crime in the moral realm, just deserts carry the added benefit of controlling the severity of punishment, since it is the subject of a rational moral reasoning to which everyone has a right of opinion.

Finally, punishing someone because he or she deserves it rather than to cure his or her illness grants the punished a certain dignity by recognizing his or her as an autonomous moral actor.

> To be cured against one's will and cured of states which we may not regard as disease is to be put on a level with those who have not yet reached the age of reason or those who never will; to be classified with infants, imbeciles and domestic animals. But to be punished, however severely, because we have deserved it, because we "ought to have known better," is to be treated as a human person made in God's image. (Lewis, 1953, p. 228)

Eighteen years later, the American Friends Service Committee (AFSC published *Struggle for Justice* (1971), in which they similarly argued against the "individualized treatment model" (or "progressive penology").[26] They too pointed out the problems inherent in therapeutic programs that end up more punitive and involving. All the "paraphernalia of the 'new' criminology" was for them just a rehashing of nineteenth-century reformist literature (AFSC, 1971, p. 8).

More recently, critics of the modern therapeutic jurisprudence movement have raised concerns over the efficacy of coerced treatment. Some scholars argue that little benefit can be derived when a client is forced into treatment, while others counter that few drug addicts would enter treatment without such external motivation and that legal coercion is no less appropriate a motivation than any other (Anglin & Hser, 1990, p. 438).[27]

Some have voiced concerns that the coercive nature of mandated therapy may enable therapists to manipulate power for their own ends and impair the development of a beneficial alliance between therapist and client, possibly preventing productive therapeutic outcomes (Anderson, Levine, Sharma, Ferretti, Steinberg, & Wallach, 1993). After all, in coercive treatment programs, the counselor ultimately works for the state, and despite a purported focus on rehabilitation, the state's interests might not always coincide with those of the client.

Alice Miller (1994) calls coerced treatment, or punishment for one's own good, "poisonous pedagogy." It teaches people to be more concerned with the punishments and rewards that result from one's behavior than the actual impact of that behavior on others. Drawing on research in child development, John Braithwaite (1999) concludes, "Punishment is a denial of confidence in the morality of the offender by reducing norm compliance to a crude cost-benefit calculation... [It] erects barriers between the offender and punisher through transforming the relationship into one of power assertion and injury" (pp. 72–73). For Braithwaite, behavior modification through punishment is problematic for any group other than, perhaps, infants. Anyone who has developed beyond these control techniques will "play the game," engaging in a crude and calculative cost/benefit analysis while in the program, only to revert back once free. Schwebel (2002) similarly argues that coerced treatment may simply lead adolescents to make an insincere commitment to abstinence. He does, however, support court-driven sanctions as an adjunct to therapy, because they lift the responsibility for sanctions off the counselor, putting it in the hands of the state.

Staff Ambivalence and Juvenile Motivation

These criticisms of coercive or correctionalist treatment have wide cultural currency, too. They draw on traditional Western concerns for the autonomy of the individual and tolerance for diversity. This tradition has endowed most Americans with a suspicion of coerced treatment, illustrated by novels such as Kesey's classic *One Flew Over the Cuckoo's Nest*, though levels of this skepticism might be waning.

In light of this tradition, it is not surprising that the counselors and court staff in the JDC themselves often had ambivalent if not conflicting attitudes toward the use of sanctions as a therapeutic tool.[28] Consistent with the concerns discussed in the literature, they were worried that relying on sanctions to ensure compliance could result in a purely "token system," that a sanction system was too rigid for dealing with different individuals, and that sanctions simply did not change the behavior of some of the youths.[29]

"You don't want them going to a totally token system," a counselor explained, "because you've got them thinking 'If I do this then there's a reward,' and there's no connection with the emotional. You know what I mean? There's no 'I'm doing this, because it's good for me.' So you don't want that too much."

"It's hard. It's very, very difficult, and it's always a struggle. Every week, every week it's a struggle... It's a very hard thing to do. It's almost like you have to have a system, and it's a struggle you know. You have to have a real system that is partially set in stone and partially individualized."

Many of the staff, not surprisingly, felt that lack of motivation was a problem for their coerced population. Comparing the JDC clients with other participants in treatment another counselor said, "And then there's the fact that they are court ordered. Motivation is not there. They pretty much are just being court compliant."

The counselor's concerns were supported by comments some of the youth made. "I just feel like I got caught with it," one youth said, "and I've got to do this. And as soon as I get off, I'll be doing it again. Next time I'll be smarter with it. I'll not be having it in my car; stay in a place and do it responsibly."

"I love weed," said another. "After I get off, I'm going to go right back to smoking it again."

The treatment staff was aware of this attitude among some of the juveniles. Another counselor said, "Well, we have to recommend [punishments] to some degree, but I think if we don't change the belief system about some of the behaviors, they're pretty much going to stay negative. But I guess that's why they come into treatment, and that's our job."

"So, you think the sanctioning works on that?"

"Yes, in some cases" (shaking head).

"You're shaking your head."

"My head is indecisive in some cases, because you have a whole range of personalities; so for some yes, and for some no."

"You think punishments work on some people?"

"It has its—yes, right... I think for some people it just really, as far as the punishment part, it just really probably adds to, as far as some of them have been punished, punished, punished, and that is all they know. And so I think it just feeds more into their feeling of hopelessness and 'Will I ever change?' or 'Will I ever get better?' We know, period, there are no black and white answers to any of this."

"Overall, I think rewards can help, and overall, there should be some type of punishment or sanctions in place; but as to it helping everyone, no. I think, well, maybe the concepts are okay, but the degree or the intensity or the types of sanction will be a governing factor as to who it helps and who it doesn't, as far as the chance of being real positive."

Drug court staff had to face the recurring problem that sanctions did not help every juvenile. Many failed the program regardless of the punishments imposed. Drug court personnel concluded that sanctions could only help those juveniles who wanted the help. The juveniles who failed in the program were simply not motivated enough to succeed.

When I asked a probation officer whether punishment "worked" she answered, "Yes, some kids, some kids it influences, and some kids it doesn't... I think it's just the kid's attitude, I guess. If they don't really care and they have an attitude where they are nonchalant or whatever, it's obviously not going to work."

Other responses mirrored this concern with distinguishing juveniles who were motivated from those who were not. "The kids who have had compliance problems are just ones who I don't think wanted to be in the program to begin with," a court member explained. "I think they thought it would be easy; it would be cake; they wouldn't really have to give up smoking marijuana."

"A lot of it is the problem of we're trying to push something on them," another court member said, "and they're not receptive to it at all."

The program succeeds with properly motivated participants—the failures simply were not motivated enough to benefit. This logic creates a paradox for coerced treatment. It only works for those who "want to be in the program," yet sanctions are implemented specifically to induce motivation among those who do *not* want treatment. The very logic of coercion assumes an unmotivated subject. Otherwise, a sanctioning system to induce compliance would not be necessary.

The lack of compliance despite sanctions poses an implicit threat to the very core of the JDC practices—the assertion that coercion helps increase therapeutic outcomes. Consequently, program failure is attributed to dispositional factors of the juveniles. The juvenile did not want to be in the program, she had a bad attitude, he was too nonchalant, and so on. This same process externalizes the failed outcome away from the program and staff and onto the juveniles. As a counselor said, "If they're not ready, they're not ready. If you've reached your maximum benefit, and that goes for adult or child—doesn't matter—if you are not ready, if you are not interested at all in doing anything to better your situation—you know, I'm not the one doing the recovery work in here. They are."

Another counselor explained, "And then in some cases, of course, like anybody, like any adult coming through here, you're not going to have the effect at all, and that's only because of choice. You have to make your own choices in life. Nobody can do it for you. And that's no reflection on the program... That's just people."

"When they're ready, they're ready," said another counselor. "It has to be a heart change. It has to come from the inside out."

Court staff also agreed. "There have been cases where there is nothing you could do," explained one court staffer. "There are some kids [for whom] this is not enough. They need to go sit in detention for a long, long time, because something didn't work early. There's a bunch of kids that it has worked for. I think it has done great things."

Another court staffer said, "I think it just depends on your mindset coming into the job... If you have the mindset where 'I can change all the kids, and I can do this and everything I say is going to go,' then you're obviously going to be disappointed."

Such attributions to the juveniles for program success and failure are in fact supported by research findings that find internal motivations for treatment (e.g., treatment readiness or responsivity) and other individual factors might be at least as important as external motivations (e.g., coercion) (Friedman et al., 1994; Smith, Subich, & Kalodner, 1995; USGAO, 2005; Cosden, Basch, Campos, Greenwell, Barazani, & Walker, 2006).

Indeed a "compelling argument" can be made that "antecedents" such as offender attributes—for example, demographics, family ties, neighborhood, prior experience in the criminal justice system, and motivation for change "may play a strong role in shaping drug court impact" (Goldkamp et al., 2001, p. 38). In fact, when Goldkamp and associates (2001) included such antecedent variables in their models to test whether participation in two different drug courts affected recidivism, the results were "not so encouraging" for proponents of drug court effects (p. 40). Almost all the purported drug court program effects disappeared when the variables were included, indicating that "prior defendant attributes" might play a larger role in future behavior than participation in the drug court program (Goldkamp et al., 2001, p. 41).

Friedman and associates (1994) found that outpatient subjects' ratings of importance of getting help significantly influenced reductions in substance use. According to some studies, "anywhere from 10% to 40% of clients' behavioral changes while in treatment can be attributed to expectation or placebo" (Lambert, 1992). It is likely that the placebo effect reflects the clients' own *decision* to change.

After its 2005 review of drug court evaluations, the USGAO concluded:

> In evaluations of 16 drug court programs in which completion was assessed, one factor—drug court program participant's compliance with program procedures—was consistently associated with program completion... No other program factor, such as severity of the sanction that would be imposed if participants failed to complete the program or the manner in which judges conducted status hearings, predicted participants' program completion. Several characteristics of the drug court program participants themselves were also associated with an increased likelihood of program completion. (p. 62)

Participants' own compliance, independent of sanctions or the hearings, predicted participant success. As Goldkamp et al. (2001) put it, in drug courts "the successes succeed and the failures fail" (p. 32).

The two most common findings for studies of coerced treatment indicate that clients entering treatment under legal coercion (1) do as well as those without such pressures and (2) sometimes remain in programs for longer periods of time than clients entering without legal compulsion (Anglin & Hser, 1990). Therefore, many researchers have concluded that coerced treatment works.[30]

This conclusion is based mostly on studies indicating that the longer a participant remains in treatment the more likely he or she is to have a positive outcome, and "time in program" has indeed been found to be a powerful predictor of treatment outcome (Anglin & Hser, 1990). Clients who stay in treatment longer are less likely to use drugs or commit crimes. Similarly, clients who terminate early from treatment report fewer therapeutic benefits and more psychological distress (Smith et al., 1995). The longer people stay in treatment, it would seem, the better off they are. So, some researchers view increased retention of clients in treatment as a positive outcome measure (Anglin & Hser, 1990).

Unfortunately, it is not entirely clear whether remaining in treatment is itself the cause of the desirable outcomes. It may not be time in the program per se that leads to positive outcomes, but rather other factors that lead to both remaining in treatment and achieving desirable outcomes. Participants who remain in treatment longer may do so, because they already wish to change their behavior. Yet the very concept of client retention so prevalent in the coerced treatment literature shifts cause from the client to the program, ignoring any client agency. It assumes, often incorrectly, that the program has retained the client, rather than the fact that the client has chosen to remain in the program.

While studying how people attempt to quit smoking, Prochaska and DiClemente (1992) identified a sequence of common stages and processes through which people attempting to change their addictive behavior typically pass *regardless* of whether their changes are self-directed or therapist directed (in a relatively non-coercive environment). Consequent research has identified five of these "Stages of Change" (Prochaska, DiClemente, & Norcross, 1992). Studying the stages of change, Smith and associates (1995) found a significant relationship between the client's stage of change before entering treatment and length of time he or she remained in the program.

> Significantly, all 9 participants in the precontemplation stage in this sample terminated prematurely from therapy, and all 15 of the participants who entered therapy in the preparation and action stages did not terminate prematurely... It seems that knowing a client's stage of change before the start of therapy may allow for the generation of a probability estimate of whether the client is likely to terminate prematurely from therapy. (Smith et al., 1995, p. 38)

Studies of coercion as the external factor rarely consider this individual motivation factor, limiting control variables to the traditional demographics of age, gender, race, and criminal justice history.

Nevertheless, after a broad review of treatment programs for alcohol abuse, Baekeland and associates (1975) wrote, "Over and over we were impressed with the dominant role the patient, as opposed to the kind of treatment used on him, played both in his persistence in treatment and his eventual outcome" (p. 305, quoted in Vaillant, 1983, p. 287). Many studies have also found that a person's posttreatment experiences are at least as important in determining outcome as pretreatment characteristics and treatment experiences. "Factors such as family stability, exposure to stressors, and social support may be better predictors of recovery than events occurring during treatment" (W. R. Miller, 1991, p. 287).

Someone motivated to change is more likely to both remain in treatment longer *and* change one's behavior. It does not necessarily follow that length of time in treatment is in itself the crucial cause of the behavior change. Rather, the participant's motivation for change *before entering treatment* may be the causal variable for both outcome effects of desirable change and time in treatment.

What remains unanswered is the role punishments play in altering one's motivation for either remaining or changing one's behavior. In fact, in light of the importance of individual factors the effect of treatment itself, much less coerced treatment, becomes an unknown quantity.

In their experiences too, the JDC staff, especially the counselors, felt that sanctions only "worked" for certain juveniles. Although they did not feel punishments changed the behavior of the recalcitrant juveniles—those for whom coercion was intended—no one questioned the necessity of punishment in the JDC. In fact, there were often calls for more punishments. Ironically, they were calls for more punishment of the most incorrigible juveniles on whom punishments were proving least effective. But though they may have doubted the therapeutic value of punishment, its value to the program was never in question.

Accountability

"You show them that there are consequences to their actions," a JDC court member explained. "My sister has a two-year-old, and I liken it to that. You have to show them there are boundaries, and a lot of kids, at least what I've seen, a lot of kids say, 'Marijuana—we're not going to get caught. It's no big deal.' But you show them hey, there's a system in place, and we have a place to put you, and we have rules that you need to follow."

As discussed in Chapter 3, the juvenile court system's traditional focus on rehabilitation has been criticized for "neglecting to impose accountability" for the crimes that brought the youth into the system to begin with (Kurlychek et al., 1999, p. 2). So in 1998, Congress provided funding for the Juvenile Accountability Incentive Block Grants Program (JAIBG—pronounced *jay-big*) through the Office of Juvenile Justice and Delinquency Prevention (OJJDP). The title has since been shortened to the Juvenile Accountability Block Grants Program (JABG). The stated goal of the JABG program is "to reduce juvenile offending through accountability-based programs focused on both the offender and the juvenile justice system" (Office of Juvenile Justice and Delinquency Program, 2007a).

> The basic premise underlying the JABG program is that both the individual juvenile offender and the juvenile justice system must be accountable... Accountability means that each offender is assured of facing individualized consequences through which he or she is made aware of and held responsible for the loss, damage, or injury perpetrated on the victim. Such accountability is best achieved through a system of graduated sanctions that are imposed according to the nature and severity of the offense, moving from limited interventions to more restrictive actions if the offender continues delinquent activities. Accountability involves a new set of expectations and demands for the juvenile justice system. The system will need to increase its capacity to develop youth competence, to efficiently track juveniles through the system, and to provide enhanced options such as restitution, community service, victim-offender mediation, and other restorative sanctions. (Office of Juvenile Justice and Delinquency Program, 2007a)

In 1998, Congress appropriated $250 million to JABG. JABG provides funds for different "program purpose areas," such as building, expanding, renovating, or operating juvenile corrections or detention facilities, hiring additional prosecutors, and "[e]stablishing drug court programs to provide continuing judicial supervision over juvenile offenders with substance abuse problems and to integrate administration of other sanctions and services for such offenders" (Office of Juvenile Justice and Delinquency Program, 2007b). (Any reference to treatment or therapy is notable for its absence.) The JDC was implemented with funds from JABG.

As mentioned earlier, rehabilitation is only one purpose of the JDC's sanctions. Like legal sanctions generally, sanctions in the JDC also serve simply as punishment for transgression. Though the rhetoric often includes references to treatment and rehabilitation, the accountability argument focuses squarely on the importance of punishment for breaking the rules. Punishment ensures just deserts for juveniles in a justice system suspected of failing to sufficiently hold them accountable for their behavior.

During the interviews, I asked the staff and juveniles how they would define accountability and responsibility.

"Someone who is accountable is someone who is accountable for responsibilities to their family, to their parents, following house rules," a counselor said. "They are accountable for following the law. That's the way I understand it."

Another counselor told me that, for the juveniles, accountability is "probably admitting that something is wrong and then they're willing to pay the price for their actions, and if they don't, then they need to be set straight. There needs to be more consequences, I think. If they can't own up to the fact that they did something wrong, then we're not getting very far with them. And a lot of them don't think they have, but by the time I am finished with them they do."

The youth tended to agree with this definition of accountability and often held themselves accountable for their behavior in my conversations with them. One of the juveniles told me that the JDC "makes us more responsible and teaches us, you know, we shouldn't have done it and not to do it again."

"I've learned to be there and deal with what I've done," said another youth, "reap what I sow, or deal with whatever they want me to deal with... I know I've done something. I must receive repercussions and consequences for that, and if I don't deal with that, who will? So it makes me take everyday consequences better, because I have dealt with something that I am guilty of."

According to the ONDCP (2002), "For young people, understanding one's place in society and learning to take responsibility for one's actions are at least as important as knowing the risks of smoking marijuana" (p. 9). A counselor explained it to me: "I would say... [responsibility] is going through with what they are supposed to—what is dished out to them—and do it the best way they can. Be responsible for their actions, that there are always consequences to pay."

"We're trying to teach these people to be responsible children and future adults," a JDC court member told me, "so we need to make sure that they know if they're supposed to go to counseling on Tuesdays, they need to insure they get to counseling. If mom told them that morning that she may be getting off late from work, well they should say, 'Mom, could you lend me a dollar twenty-five, so I can catch the bus to get there?' Or being responsible is trying to find another means of transportation to get there. Getting to know someone else in your counseling class that lives near you so you can catch a ride with them. You know, being responsible and taking initiative."

Another counselor said that responsibility is "admitting that they have a problem and being willing to make decisions to change that situation, and to begin to take care of it themselves, rather than allowing other people to take care of it."

It seemed that many of the juveniles had, in this sense, accepted responsibility and recognized the consequences of their behavior. At the least, some understood the expediency of saying so. "[I]t's my fault that I'm in this anyway," one juvenile told me. "So, I can't blame anybody for what I've done."

Similarly, another youth said, "I mean they do to you what deserves to happen. Like if you act up and stuff, then they deserve to put you on house arrest, and they do it and that's your punishment. You can't blame anybody else but yourself."

Not all the juveniles, however, were quite so agreeable to the JDC. Often their problem had little to do with their drug use so much as their lack of respect for the court, their parents, school, or just authority generally. During some prehearing meetings, the court staff would sometimes note that a juvenile's problem was not with drugs so much as it was with authority. "I don't know if he is addicted to drugs or just doesn't like doing what he is told," served as an intermittent refrain through the various meetings.

"The biggest thing I see with these kids," a court member explained, "is they come in here, and they literally disrespect their parents. They think if they want to stay out until four 'o clock in the morning, they think they can, and their parents have repeatedly tried to tell them, no. One of my biggest things I try to teach them is that, 'You are a child.' My parents were that way. They were very discipline oriented...

"And a lot of times [the juveniles'] behavior does change. The parents will comment about that, and a lot of times the kids do. I'm very, very hard on my kids; very hard. I mean when they're doing good that's great, and I always try to give them positive encouragement. But when they mess up I get the opportunity to really, really talk to them."

One such juvenile told me, "I understand that if I do mess up they do have to punish me. Like I did miss a counseling appointment once. I overslept. They tagged me with five hours of community service on the spot. I guess I can't really complain about that, because oversleeping isn't really a good excuse. Had there been other circumstances and they still gave me the five hours of community service, I probably wouldn't be too happy."

When I asked one court member what problem in the JDC she found most annoying, she replied, "a failure to follow the rules. You know, even using drugs is kind of an outstretch of that. So, it's probably that one, just failure to follow the defined conditions of the program."

Several of the youths mentioned that some of their peers did not show the proper respect for personnel in the courtroom. "I've seen other people where [the court] just takes them light," one youth said. "How can I put it in words? You know, take them lightly, you know? Don't take them seriously. Don't take their words to heart... But I can see how [court staff members] do that to some people. [The juveniles] don't show respect to the judge or something... Just not showing respect, sitting all slouched down."

I noticed this, too, during some of my court observations. Although all the juveniles were instructed to address the judge formally when speaking to the judge, some regularly failed to do so and were always corrected. Some would not sit up straight. A few times juveniles rolled their eyes while sitting in the gallery when the judge spoke to another youth.

These displays of disrespect for court personnel often gave rise to situational sanctioning from the judge.[31] The judge would sometimes lecture the juvenile for not sitting up straight or for the other behaviors that indicate a lack of proper respect in a court of law. I often found myself pleading with a juvenile in my mind. *Please, sit up straight. Stop rolling your eyes. Don't sigh when the judge says something. Please, just do what you're told.* Likewise, parents would sometimes whisper to their child to fold his or her hands on the table, or to sit up, or to address the judge more respectfully.

Time and again, I was confounded by the decisions made by some of the juveniles that only made things more difficult and further extended an unpromising process. Some of them were, simply, difficult. They were difficult in court, difficult in school, and by their own admissions difficult with family and friends. Most of the juveniles testing positive for drugs were neither dependent nor addicted. Yet, there they were facing community service, essays, additional drug tests, more treatment meetings, and more overall parental and state intrusion into their lives as a consequence of the decisions they made while in the program—positive drug tests, missed treatment meetings, and even more banal acts of disobedience like rolling their eyes and slouching in their chairs. It seemed not so much a drug treatment court as an oppositional defiant court. These defiant kids just happened to get busted with marijuana.

Recalcitrant youth were punished for failing to do what they were told, failing the treatment program, failing to take advantage of the resources provided them, and failing to recognize the value of the program and to validate the program and its staff. Sanctions did not work in the sense that they rehabilitated disobedient youth but in the sense that they punished disobedience. In this way, the program could dish out just deserts, or hold them "accountable," while citing the therapeutic benefits received by those who complied and graduated.

Finally, the punishments helped reassert the authority of the court and the individuals working within it.[32] It is the act of punishment itself that establishes when a behavior is deviant. Punishing a disobedient youth served as a means to reestablish the boundaries of acceptable behavior and the authority of the court to define those boundaries. The punishments held juveniles who violated the rules accountable to the authority of the court and the individuals working within it.

Ultimately the JDC really was, just as drug court proponents have argued, both treatment based and punishment based. Drug courts represent the compromise of two conflicting punishment ideologies. Unfortunately, a compromise among proponents does not mean the two perspectives will merge into a single cohesive system. Rather, the JDC is a patchwork of retributive and rehabilitative practices and philosophies of punishment—a crazy-quilt where the two perspectives have been stitched together as a matter of expedience more than clarity. They are part of the same blanket, but it takes a lot of needlework to hold them together.

6 | DRUG TESTING AND THE SURVEILLANCE SOCIETY

The kids know we're watching them and keeping an eye on them. It deters them from doing other things.

JDC Staff Member

If it's going to get me out of trouble, I'll pee in the cup for 'em.

JDC Juvenile

In the JDC waiting room, three mounted monitors play a video loop of the presiding judge who informs waiting parents and their kids of their rights and responsibilities regarding the impending hearing. Beneath one of the monitors next to the restroom stands a JDC probation officer with white rubber gloves and a box full of empty receptacles for urine samples. As the video judge looks out over the room, six juveniles stand in line for the restrooms, cup in hand, waiting for their turn for the bathroom. One youth comes out and gently slides the half-filled pee-cup into a small bag held open by the probation officer. The next one in line heads for the restroom.

"It keeps them clean," a counselor said. "At least helps keep them clean enough that we've got a brain to work with. I've worked at a place for many years that did not do drug testing, and, believe me, I love it here doing drug testing, because we have folks that are clean just because they don't want to go to jail or whatever. So we got some brains. We can work with something."

Several of the juveniles agreed that the tests helped keep them clean. "I think they're good, personally," one juvenile told me, "because it's helping me to stay clean."

"It's a good thing to do," a juvenile agreed. "It's a good way to keep you clean... If you don't do [drugs], then you don't have to worry about it. You don't have to worry about a drug test."

"But I don't know," he added. "Sometimes, when you don't have to pee and you have to take one and you don't take one, then it's counted dirty. That's kind of out of the question, you know. If you can't go to the bathroom, if you can't make a drop, you shouldn't be counted dirty for not having to pee." A soda machine in the stairwell going up to the courtroom does a brisk business on drug court day, as many of the juveniles buy a soda and stand in front of the waiting room, gulping down the drink to facilitate the testing process.

"It's a motivator for them to stay away from their drug of choice," another counselor said. "It gives them that specter of having to pass a drug test. And the more creative ones are going to find a way around it, but I found that the threat of having—I hate using the word 'threat,' but the prospect of having—a drug screen on a regular basis makes them think."

I asked why she hated using the word "threat."

"Well in some cases it is a threat, and that sounds pretty negative. What I try to tell my clients is that 'Yep, you're going to be drug-screened, and one way of looking at it is that if you're still using it's going to be a threat. If you're not using, it's not going to be a threat. You have nothing to hide.'"

Intensive supervision by the court is the most salient aspect of drug treatment courts. Indeed, surveillance is the very cornerstone of the correctional approach of drug courts (if not corrections generally). Juveniles' regular attendance at compliance hearings coupled with drug testing provide the framework of monitoring through which all other JDC services and punishments are delivered. Surveillance through drug testing connects treatment to punishment. According to proponents, "[a] court-ordered program must build a chain-link fence around the drug-using offender whose links consist of frequent supervision contacts and drug testing, direct access to full information on the drug offender's progress, immediate responses to program failures, and frequent progress report hearings before a single Drug Court judge and permanent staff" (Tauber, 1993, p. 11).

Quick identification of users through surveillance, it is argued, increases participant accountability and allows for early intervention and the application of predictable consequences (Torres, 1996). Supervision of these users "must be comprehensive and well-coordinated to insure offender accountability" (Tauber, 1993, p. 11).

> An accurate testing program is the most objective and efficient way to establish a framework for accountability and to gauge each participant's progress. Modern technology offers highly reliable testing to determine if an individual has recently used specific drugs... [Alcohol and drug testing] is central to the drug court's monitoring of participant compliance. It is both objective and cost effective. (National Association of Drug Court Professionals, 1997, p. 21)

To some extent, advances in drug testing technologies have made drug courts possible. At the very least, the high levels of surveillance provided at a reasonable cost by drug testing has in many ways defined the drug court process. In fact, the pervasiveness of drug testing technologies has become a fact of life for many Americans at work, home, school, and for those caught in the net, the criminal justice system.

The Drug Testing Phenomenon

The use of drug testing is by no means restricted to drug treatment courts. Most clinicians and counselors support drug testing for its clinical uses in detecting drug use and potential relapse (Anglin and Hser, 1990). Proponents argue that drug tests not only confirm and confront participant honesty about his or her drug use, but the identification of drug use provided by drug tests also allows for immediate intervention. A total abstinence policy coupled with "an aggressive and sophisticated detection program leading to certain sanctions and/or mandatory treatment for drug use," it is argued, will deter many offenders from using drugs (Torres, 2000, p. 47).

Since the 1970s, urine testing for drug use has been a routine procedure in clinical settings, especially in emergencies when drug use is suspected (Ackerman, 1991). Seen as the "simplest and most efficient tool for the diagnosis of substance abuse," it was recommended as an aid for diagnosing psychiatric outpatients (Ackerman, 1991, p. 11). As more and more outpatient and inpatient treatment programs for drug users were established throughout the country, drug screening came to be used routinely to monitor surreptitious drug use (Ackerman, 1991).

In the early 1970s, several pilot drug testing programs were introduced within the criminal justice system to monitor the drug use of offenders identified as drug dependent (Ackerman, 1991). The Special Action Office for Drug Abuse Prevention (SAODAP), the Law Enforcement Assistance Administration (LEAA), and the National Institute on Drug Abuse (NIDA) began sponsoring drug screening programs throughout the country in the hopes of controlling the criminal activity of drug-using individuals (Ackerman, 1991).

In 1977, then director of NIDA, Robert J. DuPont (1977), proposed a program for drug testing all offenders, dubbed Operation Trip-Wire, in a speech to the Federal Bar Association.

> A routine, random urine drug testing should... be used for all probationers and parolees; the average frequency of testing should be once or twice a year. Such random testing of the entire probation and parole population will serve both as a deterrent and as a case-finding technique. But the main thrust of Operation Trip-Wire is not the random testing; it is the systematic testing and follow-up of those who are known to be or have been heroin addicts. (Quoted in Wish and Gropper, 1990, p. 331)

Interestingly, this proposal, modest by today's standards, "met with considerable criticism and resistance and was a factor in DuPont's being replaced as director of the National Institute on Drug Abuse" (Wish & Gropper, 1990, p. 331).[33]

By 1989, however, the ONDCP (2002) declared that "drug tests should be a part of every stage of the criminal justice process—at the time of arrest and throughout the period of probation or incarceration—because they are the most effective way of keeping offenders off drugs both in and out of detention" (p. 26).

In a 1995 survey by the BJS, 49 percent of all probationers reported having been tested for drug use while on their current probation sentence (Mumola, 1998). Another more recent survey by the BJS found that 71 percent of all local jail jurisdictions reported having a policy to test inmates or staff for drug use (BJS, 2000). In 1999, state parole agencies reported drug testing more than 2 million adult parolees (Petersilia, 2003). Roughly 1 percent of those parolees had their parole revoked because of a positive test (Petersilia, 2003).

The JDC's county court began building its own drug testing lab within the courthouse building. Prior to this, urine samples had to be sent off to labs, and the tests were expensive, up to $25 each, depending on the lab. Lack of funding limited the number of tests in the court system to 37,000 adults and juveniles on probation or bail in 1999. Court officials hoped the new lab would be able to run 80,000 tests a year. All costs were projected to be covered by "user fees" paid by those tested.

Research, however, does not provide conclusive support for the criminal justice system's growing reliance on drug testing. When early evaluations of the large-scale 1960s' California Civil Addict Program found initial reductions in drug use among participants, the researchers attributed this success to the program's surveillance: "Because of reasonably effective monitoring by urine testing, any return to compulsive patterns of narcotics use could be identified soon after relapse and a proper intervention effected (often including a short 'dry out' incarceration)" (Anglin & Hser, 1990, p. 425). Later follow-up, however, found that only one-third of the participants saw a sustained decrease in drug use (Anglin & Hser, 1990).

Approximately one-third of the sample reached precommitment levels of drug use within three years after discharge, and the "chronic-street-addict" group, representing another third, actually exceeded precommitment use levels after discharge (Anglin & Hser, 1990, p. 426).

In 1990, a year after the first drug court was implemented in Miami, Anglin and Hser (1990), proponents of drug testing in treatment, pointed out that its effects on treatment outcome had yet to be "thoroughly studied." In a review of the literature, they concluded that "the few available treatment studies mostly found that urine testing, in the context of the overall treatment, does not improve program outcomes" (Anglin and Hser, 1990, p. 437). But they did argue that it could be effective when linked to sanctions applied to those who test positive. Wish and Gropper (1990) similarly concluded, "While it is conceivable that a program of random drug testing could deter convicted persons from drug use, no research is available regarding this topic" (p. 331).

One of the few drug court studies to utilize randomized control groups compared the recidivism rates of drug court participants with defendants in three other probation tracks. The tracks differed in the frequency of drug testing, with the drug court having the highest frequency of drug testing. Results revealed little difference in recidivism between drug court participants being tested often and defendants in the three other probation groups with little or no testing (Deschenes & Greenwood, 1994). Approximately 15 percent of probationers in the three probation tracks had new arrests after a six-month follow-up, compared to 16.9 percent of the more frequently drug-tested defendants in the drug court group (Deschenes & Greenwood, 1994). Drug court participants remained in the program longer than members of the other tracks. Participants also showed lower levels of technical violations, but much of that could be the effect of discretionary decisions made by program staff.

Turner and associates (1999) studied participant perceptions of the drug treatment court process. They conducted follow-up interviews with adult drug court participants to elicit their attitudes and perceptions of the difficulty of program compliance, the helpfulness of the drug court experience, the strengths and weaknesses of the program, and even whether they would recommend the program to other first-time drug offenders. From these closed-ended surveys, the researchers found that almost 70 percent of the (31) respondents "viewed monitoring of drug use via urinalysis tests as a strength" (Turner et al., 1999, p. 80). Of the 31 subjects interviewed by Turner and colleagues, 62 percent were successful graduates of the drug court. The most frequently cited reason for unsuccessful termination reported by the other 38 percent was positive drug tests and violating the drug court contract.

In 2002, Haapanen and Britton studied the effects of drug testing on parole outcomes for 1,958 California Youth Authority juvenile parolees. The juveniles were randomly assigned to one of five different groups varying by levels of drug testing from no testing to two tests per month. The researchers found no difference in new arrests or parole compliance between the different groups (no difference was found between ethnic or drug use history subgroups either). Two tests a month, however, is less testing than most drug courts require in the early phase, and agents were not allowed to increase testing in response to a positive drug test or to reduce testing as a reward for negative tests, as is common in drug courts.

Other studies of surveillance generally suggest that high levels of surveillance may also carry unforeseen consequences. Lepper and Greene (1975), for example, found that children who believed they were being monitored by a video camera during play showed lower subsequent interest in the play than children who believed they were not monitored. Enzle and Anderson (1993) similarly found that college students who believed they were being monitored by a video camera for evaluative purposes or to make sure they followed directions also showed less subsequent interest in the activity than subjects unaware they were under surveillance. The researchers concluded that when observation implies controlling intentions, it can undermine people's own intrinsic motivations to act (Enzle & Anderson, 1993). For the monitored subjects, surveillance represented an extrinsic attempt to control their activities.

The nonmonitored subjects, moreover, expressed "significantly greater self-perceived autonomy" than did knowingly monitored subjects, according to postexperiment self-rating surveys (Enzle & Anderson, 1993). Monitoring for controlling purposes may erode subjects' self-perceived autonomy, thus further supplanting intrinsic with extrinsic motivation (Enzle & Anderson, 1993). Research suggests that the more people believe that they have chosen something for themselves, rather than being forced, the more likely they are to succeed (Volpicelli & Szalavitz, 2000, p. 88).

This may help explain why much of the effect demonstrated under intensive supervision disappears, or even deteriorates to levels worse than before, when subjects have left the supervision of the program—the increase in drug use among some participants in the California Civil Addict Program after leaving, for instance. Though they may have stopped drug use while being closely monitored in the program, the subtle undermining of their sense of autonomy and intrinsic motivation could have led ultimately to even less self-control than before treatment.

It is worth noting that the Urban Institute found in its broad study of juvenile drug courts that some youths switched from marijuana to cocaine and LSD to avoid detection in drug tests, since those two drugs pass out of the body much faster than THC metabolites (Butts & Roman, 2004). As discussed, some of the juveniles admitted to me their intentions of using drugs once they were out of the program. By potentially undermining their own intrinsic motivations to control use, maintain good health, and succeed in school, the JDC's reliance on intensive surveillance may have undesirable side effects.

A Second Look

Some critics have made other more philosophical critiques of the reliance on drug tests and surveillance, which are pertinent to this discussion. A. Hoffman (1987), for instance, argues that drug testing is more about controlling citizens than drug use. Walsh and Trumble (1991) note that many Americans find drug testing "degrading and dehumanizing" (p. 24), though 17 years later it is not clear that still remains the case. This sentiment, however, was mentioned in some of the interviews.

"It just violates," a youth complained. "It's weird."

"What do you think is weird about it?"

"I don't think you should have to pee in a cup. I don't like doing that."

"I don't like the aiming or whatever," another juvenile said. "I'll do it 'cause you have to, but I don't like it... I can deal with it, but just like the aiming and stuff, you know. It's weird, because they stand at the door and stuff. It's a weird situation."

Another juvenile observed, "It's kinda weird givin' it to a lady."

"Why's that?"

"I wouldn't want to handle someone else's pee."

Another juvenile, concerned with more practical matters, complained "the cups are too small" resulting in splashing and spillage.

Technological advances in sweat and saliva–based drug detection tests will soon obviate these urine-specific concerns.[34] Indeed, there is no shortage of technologies for catching wayward drug users. The National Institute on Alcohol Abuse and Alcoholism has been awarding contracts to companies to develop more sophisticated instruments of continuous drug and alcohol surveillance. Such cutting-edge technologies include two devices: one that can be implanted in the body and another with a low-powered laser that could take alcohol readings by scanning one's fingers.

Global Detection & Reporting Inc. has developed the DrugWipe that can be swiped over one's furniture, computer keyboards, or skin to detect substances left behind in the minute secretions from one's skin "down to the nanogram." SpectRx is developing a skin patch that can detect alcohol in the body. Alcohol Monitoring

Systems Inc. has developed an ankle bracelet that can detect alcohol in the wearer's sweat and transmit that information to a central database through a modem. The Secure Continuous Remote Alcohol Monitor (SCRAM) "goes everywhere your clients go—24 hours a day, 7 days a week" (SCRAM, 2007).

In 1994, Gilliom warned that advances in drug testing surveillance technology may be fueling a technologically determined overreliance on these measures without consideration of their actual usefulness. In other words, drug tests are increasingly used because they are increasingly cheaper, more accurate and easier to conduct, rather than because they actually enhance treatment provision or lead to more therapeutic outcomes.

One staff member emphasized the prominence of drug testing in the JDC. "The drug tests to me are phenomenally important," she said. "[They are] the foundation... If I had nothing else but a drug test each week, I would be happy."

Drug testing, meant as a treatment tool for quick intervention with addiction relapse, is coming to be seen as treatment practically by itself. It is enough for the staffer to be able to drug test. Everything else is incidental. Increasingly, with drug testing, it seems that the means are merging with the ends.

Drug tests are not only a means to identify drug use for punishment; they also serve as the end punishment themselves. The first sanction for a positive drug test, for example, is more tests. If someone is caught with the current rate of drug tests, extra tests hardly seem necessary to identify drug use again. But that misses the point; the tests are the punishments. Surveillance has become both the means and the ends.

This focus on drug tests is an example of the criminal justice systems' increasing emphasis on information collection over other concerns, such as the effect these tests might have on the children subjected to them or on society in general; this is more evidence, perhaps, of the continuing institutionalization of "actuarial justice," which simply integrates drug tests into a broad flow of information for classifying and controlling offenders (Feeley & Simon, 1994).[35]

Such close monitoring in drug courts is justified on the grounds that, as Tauber puts it, most offenders entering the drug court are "in denial, and are there mostly to beat the system and avoid incarceration." This overriding concern with participant dishonesty is well illustrated by an advertisement in the newsletter for National Association of Drug Court Professionals' touting a saliva-based drug testing device. The advertisement admonished, "Don't be suspicious. Be certain."[36]

Identifying misbehavior need no longer be limited to verbal testimony or chance observation. Drug testing allows the court to bypass communication through dialogue and its inherent subjectivities. The tested individual simply gives up information about himself or herself.

Testing Outside the JDC

Gilliom (1994) places the growth of drug testing within "a broader reorientation of social control policy," including such things as polygraph tests, electronic bracelets, AIDS screening, genetic screening, drunk driver checkpoints, video monitoring in banks and shopping malls, and the use of widespread surveillance as a general mechanism to control crime and deviance (p. 2). Together, Gilliom argues, these policies are part of a larger disciplining of social control that requires omnipresent surveillance. Drug testing may be just one more facet of this disciplining of society.

In the disciplining society, surveillance is not limited to the prison and other facets of the criminal justice system. All institutions articulate shared means of control (Foucault, 1995). The practice of placing individuals under observation within the criminal justice system is part and parcel of a society that regularly utilizes disciplinary techniques such as testing, identification and correction of anomaly (Foucault, 1995). "Is it surprising," Foucault asks, "that prisons resemble factories, schools, barracks, hospitals, which all resemble prisons?" (p. 228).

The majority of the drug court participants told me they had already taken drug tests at home or in school before ever coming into the JDC. One juvenile with whom I spoke, for example, had been drug tested by his parents after they caught him "sneaking off." Such home drug testing kits are advertised for use by parents, athletics, small companies, and others. Indeed, concerned parents can choose from an array of home drug testing kits, available through the Internet or the local drug store, for monitoring their children.

According to Join Together Online (2003a), home drug testing kit sales have grown to more than $10 million a year since the kits were introduced in 1999.[37] Many of the juveniles had taken a drug test, unrelated to the JDC, at school. Some had to take a test to play in sports.

"I think it's a little extreme," said one youth. "Well, I mean because I take one twice a week anyway at counseling, and then here every other week, and then my school gives me a regular drug test. For me, I think it's a little much."

The number of schools drug testing students is growing. Federal funding for drug testing in schools increased 300 percent in 2003–2006 (Roan, 2007). The Bush administration has requested $17.9 million for school-based drug testing programs for 2008. Approximately 1000 schools nationwide have instituted drug testing programs (Roan, 2007).

A number of recent court cases, moreover, have broadened the powers of school districts to drug test students, leading some critics to note that "an increasing number of public school students find themselves facing another rite of passage in their public school experiences: the random urinalysis" (Hutchens, 2002, p. 1265).

In 1995, the Supreme Court upheld a school district's right to randomly drug test student athletes in *Veronia v. Acton*. The 6–3 majority opinion, written by Justice Scalia, argued that, although drug testing did constitute a search subject to the demands of the Fourth Amendment, the district's drug testing policy was reasonable under the circumstances, taking into account (1) the decreased expectation of privacy with regard to students, particularly student athletes; (2) the relative unobtrusiveness of the search; and (3) the severity of the need met by the search (*Veronia v. Acton*).

The Supreme Court, in 2002, expanded the *Veronia* decision to include all students involved in extracurricular activities, in *Board of Education v. Earls*. Another 6–3 majority argued that drug testing all students in extracurricular activities reasonably served the school district's "important interest in detecting and preventing drug abuse" and did not violate the Fourth Amendment (*Board of Education v. Earls*). The dissent, written by Justice Ginsburg, argued that the drug testing policy was not reasonable since it targeted students in extracurricular activities, a student population "least likely to be at risk from illicit drugs and their damaging effects" (*Board of Education v. Earls*, p. 43).

At the time of the decision, only an estimated 3 percent of school districts nationwide drug tested its students (Wishnia, 2002). But the *Earls* decision is still relatively recent. Reactions to *Earls* have varied widely among school districts. Some personnel have noted that drug testing all students in extracurricular activities would be too expensive, while others have concluded that students participating in extracurricular activities are the ones least likely to engage in drug use and other illegal activities (Rice, 2002; Wishnia, 2002). Testing them would make little sense and may even discourage the more "at-risk" youth from joining these conventional activities. And the sentiments of one school board president following the *Earls* decision may portend the next trend to come, "I'd hate to segregate," he said, "if they're going to test one segment, why not test everybody?" (Rice, 2002).

The ONDCP has produced a new newsletter, "Strategies for Success: New Pathways to Drug Abuse Prevention," to champion random drug testing of children. It has also developed a webpage, RandomStudentDrugTesting.org, for the same purpose, and it carries on "summits" to disseminate information to educators and parents supporting the spread to student drug testing.

The only published wide-scale study of drug testing in schools, however, has found no difference in drug use rates between schools that did drug test students and those that did not (Yamaguchi, Johnston, & O'Malley, 2003). Among 76,000 eighth-, tenth-, and twelfth-grade students surveyed in the study, school drug testing had no association with either the prevalence or frequency of marijuana or any other illicit drug use (Yamaguchi et al., 2003). Interestingly, in response to the study, the National School Boards Association announced that despite the findings schools should continue to test students (Join Together Online, 2003b).

Technologies of the criminal justice eventually bleed into other social institutions. Drug testing convicted offenders prepares people who find drug tests "degrading and dehumanizing" to accept testing unconvicted arrestees, which prepares them to accept testing misbehaving students, which leads to randomly testing all students, which is in essence a national program for regularly drug testing all children.

The youths are not the only ones being tested. It is likely that many of their parents have also been drug tested. In the interest of assuring employees are "fit to work," most major U.S. firms have some sort of drug testing for employees (American Management Association [AMA], 2001a). As part of his War on Drugs, Ronald Reagan's 1986 Executive Order 12564 required federal agencies to develop a comprehensive drug-free workplace program, including drug testing (Potter & Orfali, 1995). This was followed by the 1988 Drug-Free Workplace Act, which required federal grantees and contractors with contracts of $25,000 or more to ensure a drug-free workplace (Potter & Orfali, 1995). Since then, the annual National Drug Control Strategies have defended and proselytized for workplace drug testing.

In 1988, a Gallup survey found that 28 percent of the nation's largest companies used drug testing to screen applicants (Ackerman, 1991). By 2001, a survey by the AMA found that 67 percent of major U.S. firms drug tested employees. According to the AMA (2001a), "Drug testing is, in fact, the primary factor in workplace medical testing."[38]

For juveniles, though, school is by far the most important center of surveillance technologies. Many had been caught with marijuana at school. Several of the juveniles told me about drug sniffing dogs being brought into their schools. "I went to school and I had a couple of roaches of pot in my car," a youth told me, "and they had drug dogs checking the parking lot."

Some of these school busts were part of the school district's new program that, in conjunction with the police department, paid students $50 to turn in their classmates for drug offenses. "Like, say Billy knows Sandy has drugs," a youth who had been busted through the program explained to me, "Billy can tell on Sandy. She gets busted, and he gets fifty bucks."

"So somebody made fifty bucks off your arrest?"

"It's a lot. People go around doin' it a lot. They save up money when they do that."

"It's gotten so out of control with the kids and marijuana," a JDC court staffer said, "that a kid can be walking down the street or down the hallway, and someone just throws something at him. And there's the police officer. The kid may be totally innocent. Kids set each other up all the time. They set up a kid, and they call the Crime Stoppers because they get $50."[39]

"My lawyer says somebody [turned me in], but they won't tell me who," one juvenile busted at school told me. "Somebody got paid."

"What do you think about that?"

"I don't like it, because he said it was one of my family members that snitched on me."

* * *

The value of intensive surveillance has been largely taken for granted in drug court practices. The research on drug testing, however, has not effectively demonstrated what, if any, role it plays in therapeutic outcomes. In fact, the heavy reliance on surveillance may reflect a broader orientation toward increasing institutional supervision and control of individuals more so than demonstrated treatment benefits. Such a possibility deserves the attention of research on the impacts of drug courts.

Placing the growth of drug testing within a broader context further raises questions as to whether the reliance on surveillance is driven more by technology and larger social movements than the inherent value it has as a treatment tool. Moreover, from an evaluative standpoint surveillance may have untoward effects on the objects monitored. It may decrease intrinsic motivation and sense of autonomy or it may simply engender a sense of mutual distrust as open communication and its risks (and benefits) are replaced by the science of surveillance. Evaluations of drug courts should explore these qualitative outcomes as very real possibilities in the drug court process.

7 | SUCCESS

So what I look at being success is maybe seeing some kind of a seed that's beginning to grow... When I see the seed after it's been planted, and it begins to grow because they're watering it with knowledge, I know there's going to be a good outcome.

JDC Counselor

I want to get out of trouble.

JDC Juvenile

Despite the often critical tone of this book, the youth in the JDC did report benefits from the program. The staff also felt they were helping most of them. There were, in other words, beneficial outcomes. What remains unclear is whether the JDC practices of focusing on the juveniles' "denial," punishing, and drug testing were the catalysts for these benefits.

Generally, a successful drug court participant is one who follows the rules of the program, attends the required treatment meetings and courtroom hearings, turns in clean drug tests, progresses through the treatment phases, does not get rearrested, finally graduates from the program within a specified time span, and has the original charges dismissed or expunged. As a JDC court member put it, a successful participant is "one that abides by our rules and never gets in trouble and goes to counseling and goes to school and does good in school."

In the first year of the JDC, about 30 percent of the juveniles were terminated from the program. Just over 25 percent of the participants reoffended.[40] Only 12 percent of all the drug tests were positive. What was the "success rate" for the program? 70 percent, 75 percent, 88 percent? What is "success"?

Goldkamp and Weiland (1993) have noted the difficulty of defining success in drug treatment courts. They point out that from the criminal justice perspective, reduced recidivism measures success, but from the treatment perspective, compliance and retention are the primary indicators of success. Others might argue that personal responsibility and autonomy, well-being, and health are good outcomes to be desired. The OJP (2001) lists a number of other program benefits some of the juvenile participants may experience such as community volunteering, increased involvement in writing or music, increased involvement in church/faith group activities, and so on.

Some participants unsuccessfully terminated from the program may nevertheless control their drug use and stop other criminal activity, cultivate greater "responsibility," learn accountability lessons, improve in school, or make other positive life changes on their own later. On the other hand, some graduates may be rearrested, feel labeled as drug addicts, lose their sense of autonomy, or increase unhealthy drug use patterns.

In practice, both participants and staff have their own definitions of success and identify their own benefits and costs associated with the program. In our interviews, most of the juveniles identified at least one benefit they felt they had received from the program. Primarily, almost all mentioned getting their charges dropped as the top benefit. Some also said they were stopping or reducing their drug use, doing better in school, or getting along better with friends and family. Some saw no benefits from the program, and a couple even said they felt worse off. A discussion of these perceived benefits follows.

Getting Charges Dropped

Success for one juvenile was "not to get any violations on anything and make sure I do all the things I'm supposed to do. Go to all of my counseling sessions and try to get through it all," so that his charges would be dropped and he could leave the experience behind him.

It is perhaps not surprising that most of the juveniles said getting their charges dismissed was the biggest benefit of the program. Almost all of them cited this as the primary reason they opted into the JDC. Some even said it was the only benefit they anticipated receiving from the program. In light of the obstacles and restrictions faced by individuals convicted of drug crimes, this makes sense. To some extent, though, this benefit of the JDC was overstated. As juveniles, their records are closed when they reach adulthood anyway. Still, for the majority of participants, success meant avoiding going through life with the drug charge on their record, closed or not.

Stopping Drug Use

In addition to a clean criminal record, some said that quitting marijuana was a benefit. One youth told me he was glad to be in court, "so I can get away from [marijuana]. I mean, I'm just glad that I got caught now instead of later when I had, you know, more stuff on me, and, I don't know." The youth said that a successful outcome was "staying away from all drugs." Another put it succinctly, "to just quit drugs."

One juvenile who said he smoked marijuana to keep himself occupied found that pot was taking over too much of his life. "That's why I'm glad this all happened," he said, "because I felt like everything revolved around marijuana. Everything I did. Got to smoke a joint before I go to school. Leave to go smoke. Now it's like you go to school to learn."

Improving School Performance

In fact, several of the youths rediscovered the subtle joys of going to school sober. "Before this, I didn't even know what it was like to be in high school and not be a pot smoker," a juvenile told me. "It's not like a difficult thing. I still have some of my old friends. And yes, they still smoke weed. And no, I'm not around them when they do it. It helped me find out which of my friendships were based on smoking weed and which were actual friendships."

"Like now we have to maintain like our school grades and stuff," said another juvenile. "So I need to focus on my schoolwork, and like last semester I just goofed off, because I didn't think it would bother anything. But this semester I've buckled down on school, and like I don't go out with my friends every night like I used to. I stay home and I study." The benefit of higher academic achievements for many juveniles meant they had found success in the program.

Personal Relations

Many juveniles mentioned benefits only indirectly related to drugs. This should not be surprising, since most of them simply did not have terribly acute drug habits. It is sometimes easy to assume that drugs play a larger role in the lives of drug court participants because they are, after all, in a drug court, where drug use has come to serve as their primary identifier. But as discussed, most of the juveniles used marijuana only occasionally and did not use other drugs, like alcohol, much at all. So it makes sense that they would find benefits only peripherally related to drugs, since drugs played only a peripheral role in their lives.

In fact, one juvenile who was quite critical of the court's approach to treatment still found the treatment meetings beneficial. "I guess [the treatment meetings] are just an opportunity to talk... I don't really like them as far as talking about drugs, but it does give you a small group to kind of open up to and talk to... It's just a nice feeling to be able to go to a group like that."

Another juvenile said the treatment meetings helped him to better manage his anger. "Before I got arrested, I didn't listen you know, argumentative... I'm still a little bit argumentative, but I got anger control. I still have anger, but I'm working on that."

Some of the juveniles even felt that meeting the program's rigorous requirements had brought them and their parents closer. Speaking of his father, one youth said, "He never really took me any place or anything, and now he sometimes brings me up here and sometimes brings me to [treatment] classes, and I get to talk to him in between about this stuff."

"I think it has brought me and my dad closer," said another youth. "I think we talk more. He used to not tell me what his kid life was like and what type of drugs he used to do, but now it's like he has brought it all out."

One juvenile told me he had grown closer to his mom out of their shared frustration with the JDC program.

One youth who intended to resume smoking after leaving the program nevertheless felt she had benefited from the program, because it led to spending time with a new group of friends. "If I hadn't [come through the program]," she stated, "I'd probably be hangin' out with some of the same people that I was three months ago, and they were losers."

Similarly, another youth explained, "I'm hanging out with some of my friends that I had stopped hanging out with. I'm getting along better with my dad. I talk to my brothers and sisters more now."

These benefits, though peripheral to drug use, translated into successful experiences within the program, because the juveniles felt they left the program with their lives changed positively in some way.

No Benefits

There were some youth who felt they had not benefited much from the program at all. I asked one youth whether he felt like he was better off for having come through the drug court. "No," he replied.

"Why is that?"

"I feel like I just got caught with it."

"Do you feel like you're worse off?"

"No. I just feel like I got caught with it, and I've got to do this, and then as soon as I get off, I'll be doing it again. Next time I'll be smarter with it."

Another juvenile shared a similar sentiment stating that a successful outcome was, "not to get caught. Not only that, but just to be more careful about what I do."

For these youth, success was learning how to avoid future police/court intervention.

Some said they felt worse off. These juveniles usually included the fallout from the arrest when considering the effects of the JDC on their lives. One such juvenile said he felt worse off, partly for having been arrested and consequently kicked out of school and partly for entering the drug court "because now I'm not in school, and I don't have a social life with my friends. And it makes me like closed-down to everybody else. Like, when I did go to school, and I did smoke weed or whatever, I could still sit down and talk to everybody, and now I don't want to talk to nobody."

Change

Identifying success can sometimes be difficult. It may be viewed restrictively as a dichotomous outcome: one is either a success or a failure in drug treatment. Success might simply connote a static condition without considering one's progress relative to one's own starting point and individual goals (Stahler, Cohen, Greene, Shipley, & Bartelt, 1995). The JDC treatment counselors, however, tended to view change in the youths as the primary indicator of success. Each youth came into the program in a unique situation, and the counselors often tried to measure success relative to that situation. One counselor described a successful juvenile as "someone who begins to address their own issues and begins to open a door to see a different point of view. A beginning is a successful thing... A beginning starts with a different way of thinking, kind of opening the door to something new, a new way of life or a new thought pattern."

Another counselor, reluctant to use the word "failure" or "unsuccessful" for juveniles terminated from the program, shared those sentiments on the importance of change, saying, "I guess less successful or a failure in my eyes would be showing no changes, same attitude, same posture, same everything as when they came." More specifically, the counselor followed up with the hope that "the changes would for them to be able to grasp, maybe, some of the concepts of what addiction is, grasp the accountability, that their behavior does affect other people."

Change is a rather ambiguous concept. One can change in many ways, and some of those ways can be difficult to measure. For the JDC staff to identify successful change, the participant must follow a particular direction toward less drug use and the recognition that drug use is wrong. A member of the court said that success was "broader" than simply giving up drugs.

"I think probably you would define a really successful person as one that has learned the reason why it is a bad idea to use drugs, the reason why it is a bad idea to break the law, the reason behind why they have to be responsible for their own behavior, which I think is ultimately the most important element."

A treatment counselor suggested success might entail simply getting juveniles to "see that what they did was wrong" and show they're "willing to make some changes. That's success. Because my time frame and all the changes I'd like to see isn't their time frame, and I can only do so much. And they can only make so many changes at once. So, I see success as just maybe changing a perspective or an attitude."

When I asked the judge whether abstinence from drugs was necessary to consider a youth a success, the judge replied, "Yeah, as a judge it has to be." Then thinking about it more, added, "Well, that's a really hard question, because as a judge you can't really tolerate breeches in the court orders, that's pretty black and white."

But then again, the judge observed, "Life isn't really black and white. So, if a kid has learned some of the other things we have talked about, like responsibility and accountability, and they're going to school, and they're not getting arrested, and they're telling their parents where they are, and they're doing all of those other things... then it would be hard not to consider them successful to a great degree. So maybe there are degrees of success, but I think that in order to really consider them a successful person in the drug treatment program, they have to stop using."

This raises the question of the extent to which complete abstinence from drugs is required for a juvenile's program success. All drug treatment courts require a certain length of abstinence from illicit drugs and alcohol to graduate successfully from the program. This time span varies but is usually a minimum of a couple months with no positive drug tests. And many professionals in the field feel that unless complete abstinence from all drugs can be achieved, treatment is essentially a failure (Anglin & Hser, 1990). Even proponents of moderate drinking for adults insist that a period of abstinence is necessary for the individual to effectively evaluate his or her relationship with the drug (Kishline, 1994).

This raises a distinction between long-term and short-term abstinence. One counselor addressed this question of short-term abstinence from a very practical level stating, "I have to have a clean, clear mind to work with that person, and if they are under the influence or coming off of [a drug], then you are not dealing with that."

Most of the court personnel viewed total abstinence as an ideal toward which they strove to bring each juvenile closer. Another counselor explained it to me: "I would consider it pretty cool if somebody didn't use again. And then at 21 they could reevaluate maybe the drinking... That's just the most ideal—what I would always think of first.

"So many of them, they're not addicts. They got into bad situations, and they did ridiculous things, and they can change that. So I would say for the teenagers, and before they turn 21, abstinence is definitely the way to go, because they are not able to make a decision yet about those things, because they have been in trouble with it before. It has caused them problems in the past... At 21 maybe you want to reevaluate the drinking thing.

"However, I don't think it is ever alright for anybody to reevaluate and socially use illegal drugs because I don't believe in that. I don't believe you can socially use those drugs without getting into trouble. I think it always catches up with you."

Success versus Outcome

Few would argue against the benefits of reduced recidivism for both the juveniles and the community. Nonetheless, interviews with the juvenile participants and staff revealed a multitude of alternative possible benefits. One important theme I noticed in my experience with the court is that termination from the program did not preclude gaining benefits from it.

"We've even had a kid who was removed from the drug court program in Phase 2, because he was picked up on a dealing charge," a JDC staff member told me. "He just left for Boy's School this morning, because of the amount of drugs he had. At the same token, he did say he learned a lot, and he was just in the car with the person at the wrong place and the wrong time. And that's why a lot of kids get in trouble, because they're at the wrong place at the wrong time."

I spoke with some of the juveniles who were terminated from the program. Most of them felt they had received some benefits from the program. They were controlling their use. They were doing better in school. They felt closer to their parents. They showed some signs of the changes, which the counselors continually talked about. On the one hand, they experienced successes. On the other, they were kicked out for new charges or positive drug tests.

I also spoke with many juveniles who graduated from the program "successfully." But, just as termination may not preclude success, graduation did not guarantee it. Some told me they found little benefit in the program other than getting their charges dismissed. Of course, this in itself is a success, especially in light of current social and professional restrictions on drug law offenders.

A JDC staff member explained that some of the regular probation officers did not like the JDC program "because this program was supposed to weed out the case load, you know, lower the case load of those who are in probation. But... kids are leaving this program and going back to [probation's] programs and their case loads are still staying the same. They're not getting anything beneficial. Some kids skate right through the program, and they're seeing them come back right after their charges are dismissed for the same things they were in the program for."

It would seem that "success" can be found right alongside "failure," rather than in opposition to it. Success can be many things other than reduced recidivism or abstinence from drugs. A juvenile may be terminated from the JDC and still have grown closer to a parent or made new friends in the program. A juvenile may graduate from the program, but in the process may also have internalized a label of "addict" or "incorrigible" or felt an erosion of personal autonomy through the intensive surveillance. Some of these outcomes may directly counteract the purported aims of therapeutic outcomes, healthy lifestyle changes, and teaching responsibility. Even seeming success, as we have seen, may carry its own set of problems. What the findings of the book criticize is the assumption that these benefits resulted from the drug court components of the disease model, punishment, and surveillance that characterize both adult and juvenile drug courts.

8 | THE FUTURE

Cure sometimes, heal often, support always.

Hippocrates

The Widening Net

In the first year, there was already growing interest among some of the staffers in lengthening the program. One JDC staffer explained to me: "I know adult drug court has a year program. I'm a fan of that. I know that some people might not be. I think the longer you can get them to go without marijuana the better, especially since a lot of those kids stumble in those twelve weeks if they were serious marijuana users or if they have marijuana influences.

"We had a kid come in a couple of weeks ago who said, 'All my friends smoke marijuana. What do you want me to do?' We decided she should be on informal home detention, and then she won't see her friends. It's a serious problem. If they stumble at six weeks and you graduate them at 12 weeks, I just don't think they get a sense of accomplishment...

"I hate when after the program they do something else, because it's just hard to teach them that quick. I can't train my dog in 12 weeks. Not that I'm comparing a child to a dog, but I don't have a child, I have a dog. It's hard to train anybody anything in 12 weeks."

Informal home detention, generally withheld as a final punishment for noncompliance before detention in the JDC, was used as a treatment tool in its own right. It could prevent juveniles from interacting with unsavory characters and put them under higher levels of surveillance from their parents and under more control of the court.

The girl who was put on informal home detention also explained to me how it happened.

"Well, I went to court," she said. "[The judge] asked me, like, who all that I knew smoked weed or whatever. I told [the judge] everybody in my neighborhood, pretty much. So [the judge] just wanted me to stay away from the neighborhood for a little while. So [the judge] put me on [in]formal house arrest...where I have to stay with one of my parents at all times. I can't leave without my mom or dad or a guardian... It's boring. It sucks."

There is a slow creeping of increasingly intensive measures in the program. Within less than a year of the JDC's implementation, some staff were campaigning to lengthen the program. Informal home detention, in the spirit of drug courts' continuing conflation of treatment and punishment, began to morph from a punishment for noncompliance to a prevention tool.

The very existence of the juvenile drug court itself is in fact evidence of a broader creeping effect. Originally designed to treat adult hardcore addicts whose drug problems led to other crimes, the drug court model is now applied, in modified form, to juveniles arrested for marijuana possession—some of whom are not even diagnosed with a drug problem independent of the arrest itself. When researchers with the Urban Institute asked officials at juvenile drug courts about the drug use behavior of the participants in their drug court programs, "[t]he consensus view was that 80 to 90 percent of the youth referred to juvenile drug courts were *nondependent users of alcohol and marijuana*" (Butts & Roman, 2004, p. 16 [emphasis added]).

Butts and Roman (2004) further note that an estimated 2.5 million teens between the ages of 14 and 17 have used an illegal drug (almost entirely marijuana) at least once in the past 30 days, meaning that almost "2 million juveniles would test positive for illegal drugs at any given time" (p. 17). It is worth mentioning that this is a considerably lower number of kids than in the recent past, and most of those kids did quite well without judicial supervising of their lives. Both the National Drug Court Institute and National Council of Juvenile and Family Court Judges, nevertheless, have recommended eligibility criteria that could in essence include all youths who even drank alcohol (Butts & Roman, 2004).

Drug courts are also shifting the emphasis of eligibility criteria toward more "responsive," "suitable," "compatible," or "redeemable" populations (i.e., those most likely to succeed in the program and thus those least likely to need it). This could mean that serious offenders with real addiction problems will be increasingly avoided by drug courts and incarcerated. Meanwhile, more and more moderate users with a questionable need for such resource-intensive coerced treatment will comprise an increasing bulk of the clients in such programs (Curtis, 2002). Such a situation would divert scarce resources away from those who most need them and increase governmental intrusion into the lives of those who might not.

Diversions

In 1996, two out of three police chiefs surveyed favored court-supervised treatment over prison for drug abusers (Huddleston et al., 2005). It is the perception of drug courts as a less expensive, more productive alternative to incarceration that has led many to support drug courts, but there is scant evidence that youth (or adults for that matter) referred to drug courts would have been incarcerated otherwise. Most likely, they would have gone to regular probation, which requires less intensive surveillance and lower costs.

As discussed in Chapter 4, for example, the judge tried to avoid terminating juveniles specifically because they would be sent to probation, which was viewed as "the easy way out." A review of drug court outcome evaluations shows that the control groups for comparison tend to be probationers—on those occasions, that is, when the evaluations do not use the inappropriate group of drug court failures for comparison. Implicit in this choice of control group is that the individuals closest to drug court participants are probationers, not offenders recently released from prison. Most juvenile (and often adult) drug court participants are not being diverted from prison, but from probation.

In response, probation might be getting a little more intense as it is forced to compete for clients, resources, and policy priority. A JDC counselor told me about a participant in one of his treatment groups who attended treatment as a condition of probation, "Like the next group I have here, there's one guy in there who smoked pot once in his life and he drank once and got sick.... Because he mentioned that he had smoked pot that makes him eligible [for treatment]." Increasing the intensity of supervision is becoming the practice de rigueur in noncustodial programs.

The JDC is not diverting youth from detention; it is sending probation-bound youth to a more intensive and more expensive version of court-monitored probation. Meanwhile, those originally headed for detention continue to go. This is an increasingly expensive way to deal with 15-year-olds who smoke pot.

M. Kay Harris (1991) argues that the conditions of nonincarcerative penalties now demand more obedience, are more intrusive, and carry more conditions than ever before. "Just as the velvet glove only thinly cushions and screens the iron fist," she writes, "it is important to recognize that the 'velvet ankle bracelet' and its ostensibly more benign brethren 'community penalties' are facilitating the diffusion and expansion of social control through the penal system and augmenting the iron bars rather than replacing them" (pp. 86–87). Rather than an alternative to traditional adjudication, drug courts might be serving only as supplements to expanding control systems.[41]

In 1973, Hal Pepinsky (2006) warned against "diversion" programs, arguing that every new institution has in fact been a diversion from another institution. But the old institutions do not lose their populations; the new institutions simply add to the number of people being institutionalized.

> ...and as the new institutions develop a new class of people a new class of people begins to be brought in, of people we previously couldn't reach but we now discover can really benefit from the kind of service we offer. You get a new kind of person being brought under state supervision, and in addition I think you begin to set up a cycle of failure: as you begin to supervise a person, as you begin to treat a person, you provide a new regimen that the person can fail in addition to failing by committing a statutory offence and so get fed back into the system. You engender a new kind of recidivism; you expand failure. (Pepinsky, 2006, pp. 12–13)

Proponents of this expansion argue that it is a good thing to bring more people into treatment. Increasing the number of people processed through state institutions is not in and of itself inherently bad, especially if much-needed services are being provided to individuals who otherwise would not receive them. What is lacking, however, is any concerted effort to uncover what the downsides to this policy might be.

The current attitude toward drug courts presupposes the treatment program, although (and in fact because) it relies heavily on punishment and surveillance, leaves everyone subjected to it better off—as if calling something therapeutic just makes it so. The problem is that the current approach, built on an extreme view of the disease model, punishment, and intensive surveillance, may not actually be improving matters. The successful juveniles might have been doing quite well on their own anyway, and the "unsuccessful" juveniles were simply subjected to more punishments than they would have received in traditional probation.

Where it does not seem to help, there are calls for more of the same. Juveniles who violate in spite of sanctions are sanctioned more. If they are not complying in treatment, they are required to attend more treatment meetings. If they test positive for drugs, then more drug tests. The punishments are not punishing enough. The program needs to be longer to treat those it is failing to treat within the current time span. All of this and any discussion of how these practices may have any potential for harmful side effects is practically nonexistent.

The challenge to policy is to balance the potential harms of marijuana use among the juveniles with the potential harms and benefits from such intensive intervention. Take heed of the caveat: First, do no harm. Along these lines, the findings of this book would suggest that, instead of continuing the expansion of surveillance and punishment-based coercive treatment programs, we should consider slowing things down and taking stock. Less really may be more.

Rather than lengthening the JDC, for example, it might be more effective to shorten it. Research on treatment for adolescents suggests that, generally speaking, it is "better to start with the shorter, kinder program" (Volpicelli & Szalavitz, 2000, p. 91). Most reviews of research on the relative effectiveness of more versus less intensive treatment have concluded that more costly approaches evidence no better overall outcomes than less costly alternatives (W. R. Miller, 1991, p. 287). As a rule, "It almost always makes sense to try the least intensive option first" (Volpicelli & Szalavitz, 2000, p. 86).

Harm Reduction: A Policy for Now

The admonishment to *First, do no harm* is the backbone of the growing harm-reduction approach. Proponents of harm reduction aim to balance the potential dangers of drugs with the untoward side effects of drug policy (Rosenbaum, 1996). It blends a pragmatic public health approach to drug use with a concern for human rights (International Harm Reduction Association, 2007). Erickson, Riley, Cheung, and O'Hare (1997) identify several characteristics of harm reduction: (1) a value-neutral view of drug use; (2) a value-neutral view of the drug user; (3) focus on the problem; (4) the user's role in harm reduction; and (5) the irrelevance of abstinence. I consider three of these characteristics of harm reduction in light of the preceding research on the JDC.[42]

Focus on Problem

Harm reduction focuses on problems individuals face that threaten them most and inhibit fulfillment of their lives. "To establish effective harm reduction strategies... requires, from a health-promotion viewpoint, devising ways to improve living conditions, increase autonomy, improve access to services as well as provide information" (Beauchesne, 1997, p. 33).

Some of the juveniles did indeed have problems, sometimes related, often unrelated, to their drug use. Many counselors brought up a score of issues, aside from drug use and abuse, which they focused on during treatment sessions. "I try to work on their self-esteem issues," a JDC counselor told me, "get them more hopeful, try to tap into their resentments. They've got a lot of resentments, not only toward their family, toward the legal system, toward adults, authoritative figures."

Twelve percent of the youths were diagnosed primarily with "behavioral disorders," and there may be problems at home when a juvenile participant feels the JDC has brought him closer to his father, because they talk more on the way to drug treatment, or when a mother reports her son to the police to "scare him straight" and is then surprised—indignant even—to hear he must go to court.

Almost every staff member of the JDC identified family issues as representing the juveniles' most urgent needs, but only a couple of the youth or their parents were provided with any sort of family counseling or services. A few were ordered to go for counseling.

It is not very important whether the families really were the "biggest problem"; however, it is noteworthy that the JDC did not directly deal with the problem every staff member believed to be the biggest problem. Of course, a court-based program must, by definition, focus on the legal issue of drug use rather than perceived family problems, but this helps underscore the limitations of treatment in this criminal justice context.

"We have talked about that at staffing," said a counselor, "trying to get them there again. So Mom is saying, 'Okay, I will go to those stupid classes, if you will work a part-time job. Who is going to put bread on the table?' and all of that.

"Say you've got a kid that has got to come to court once every two weeks and then every single week they have to go to counseling at least once a week, sometimes twice, sometimes three times. Their parents are trying to work; the kids are in school. We try to order family counseling on top of that, in addition to that. You really need a special case in order to make it something that the families can handle."

"Some parents do need parenting skills," another JDC court member told me. "I remember I had one family, the mom had just recently been released from prison just two years prior to this complaint. Her son was born in prison, so she had only had her son for 2 years, and he was 13 years old. He had 11 years without his mom, and all of a sudden he is living with this woman he doesn't know, and she's wondering where all these problems are coming from. She never learned to be a parent to this child because she was never there. That's the thing with the lack of parenting. I always try to ask [the counselors if] they have any family counseling or parenting classes these parents could possibly take."

The TOPS study discussed in Chapter 5 found that treatment clients referred by the criminal justice system were significantly less likely than others to receive any other available services beyond drug treatment. This may be inevitable in a legalistic approach to drug treatment, where the central concern for the law is obedience. Analysis further revealed that legally referred clients received considerably fewer medical, psychological, or family services than other clients. Outpatient drug-free clients with no criminal justice involvement were twice as likely to receive three or more types of services as were TASC clients (Hubbard et al., 1988). Almost a third of the legally referred clients received none of the services available, and this despite the fact that criminal justice clients remained in treatment longer than noncriminal justice-referred clients (Hubbard et al., 1988). Results such as these cast further doubt on the ability of the legal system to address issues outside the domain of enforcing abstinence.

There is some evidence, however, that these sorts of supplementary services can in fact improve drug treatment outcomes. One study found that only 9 percent of teens given 6 months of supportive drug counseling were abstinent at the end of the study, but 73 percent of the teens receiving help with poor family and peer relationships in addition to "empathetic behavioral therapy" were abstinent at 6 months (Volpicelli & Szalavitz, 2000, p. 227). Additional evidence suggests, "[t]he best programs emphasize a broader health-consciousness and skills for personal decision making" (Kleiman, 1992, p. 22).

Client-Driven Treatment

Many of the juveniles in the JDC recognized and wanted to deal with problems in their lives, even though they did not necessarily feel their drug use was a problem. Often, an individual's apparent lack of motivation to address what someone else perceives as a drug problem may really indicate a motivation to work on other more pressing problems as the user sees them (Denning, 2000, p. 41). Perhaps the most direct means of addressing each juvenile's problems is to allow the juvenile to identify those problems for himself or herself. This is indeed the driving philosophy of most noncoercive counseling practices. Robert Schwebel (2002) points out, however, that though most counseling professionals would argue that they are not in the business of telling clients what to do, in alcohol and drug abuse treatment, counselors have most noticeably deviated from this tradition.

By far, the juveniles most appreciated the times when they could talk in treatment, usually about issues other than drug use. One of the juveniles who did not like the treatment meetings nonetheless said he did enjoy the meetings when the counselor "let us talk and see how we feel and stuff. That's the time that was good."

"It's been educational at times," another juvenile said, "although sometimes it's been just kind of too finger pointing."

It is generally assumed the outcome goals (the "key indicators" of reduced drug use and recidivism) identified by staff and policy-makers are also the best outcomes for the participants. In his critique of the rehabilitative ideal, Francis Allen (1981) warns "[w]hen what is good for the offender is exclusively determined by the state... destructive consequences are likely to follow. Lines between therapy and repression tend to fade" (p. 47). In many programs, institutional goals become conflated with participant goals. What is good for the program is good for the client.

While some drug users may not identify their substance use as a problem, they may still be willing to talk about other problems in their lives (Denning, 2000, p. 58). "People with substance use disorders should be offered treatment that is respectful of *their* assessment of their own problems and needs, and clinicians must be willing to work on areas of concern to clients that may or may not correspond to their own" (Denning, 2000, p. 8 [emphasis in original]). Discovering and addressing these problems as identified by the user himself or herself is the objective of harm reduction.

In client-driven treatment, the treatment provider tries to offer what he or she can at the moment and stands by while clients live their lives outside of the treatment meetings (Denning, 2000, p. 25). This means clients will make choices with which the treatment providers do not agree. According to some harm reduction proponents, treatment providers must remain somewhat unattached to the treatment outcome and try to avoid imposing their own biases and definitions of success on the user. For them, it is only by encouraging autonomy over one's life that responsibility for one's health can be cultivated.

True responsibility and accountability may only be possible when users are allowed to define their own goals (Denning, 2000). The World Health Organization (1998) defines health promotion as the process of enabling people to increase control over and improve their own health. It entails increasing a person's autonomy over his or her own health decisions—in other words, taking responsibility. But for the JDC, this approach to responsibility does not wash with the institutional demands for compliance with the law. Whether someone is violating or following the law is, for the court, definitive of "responsibility." Arguably, however, responsibility cannot be imposed on people; rather, it must be granted.[43]

Adolescents may benefit most from simple dialogue and inte-raction (Schwebel, 2002, p. 15).

"I have since learned that it's not a fix-it type thing," explained a JDC counselor. "I think the more we can educate and change a person's belief system rather than the behaviors and begin to get them to buy into the fact of changing their belief system to a more positive and hopeful one and if they can really just buy into that and tap into that, then the behavior modifications automatically come."

Though this comment assumes that the juveniles do not cur-rently have a "positive and hopeful" belief system based simply on the fact that they were picked up by the police or because they smoke marijuana, it does represent a counselor beginning to try to let go of a "fix-it" mentality.

"I try as hard as I can to treat those people with dignity and with respect," another counselor said. "It seems to work much better. I don't take much credit. I give it my best shot. I believe very strongly when they're ready, they're ready. It has to be a heart change; it has to come from the inside out."

Letting Go of Abstinence

Harm reduction focuses on decreasing risk and severity of poten-tial adverse consequences of use without necessarily decreasing the actual level of consumption (Single, 1997). The prohibitionist discourse behind demands for abstinence can often lead to preven-tion or treatment programs "that constitute social-control activities, rather than health promotion..." (Academic Improve-ment and Teacher Quality Programs Unit [AITQ], 1996; referred in Beauchesne, 1997, p. 38). Thus, a "logic of social control" permeates many types of treatment interventions required to con-form to legal norms. Schwebel (2002) argues, "The mad rush for abstinence that characterizes adolescent drug treatment tends to evoke either dishonesty or resistance in young people. It leads the counseling far astray of its mission to help individuals make deci-sions for themselves, and it lends to poor outcomes" (p. 16). In most prevention programs, whether treatment or education, juveniles are given the contradicting message that, although they must take responsibility and make their own decisions about drug use, they must always say "no" (Rosenbaum, 1996, p. 10).

As discussed, the JDC staff themselves noted that abstinence was not necessary to consider a juvenile "successful" in the program. Rather, positive change, improvement in school, a better understanding of the possible consequences of drug use, and other outcomes were all mentioned as indicators of success in the JDC.

Research demonstrates that programs teaching moderation are at least as successful as abstinence-focused treatments in reducing drinking and related negative consequences (Volpicelli & Szalavitz, 2000, p. 49) and often leads to higher rates of compliance and improvement than abstinence only (W. R. Miller, 1985). In fact, most people who start out in moderation programs actually come to choose abstinence on their own. But they make the decision on their own, increasing their chances for successfully achieving their goals (Volpicelli & Szalavitz, 2000, p. 88).[44]

The JDC juveniles' claims to start being smarter about where they smoke marijuana, to not get caught, to be more careful, to not take it to school may all indicate successful behavioral modifications to reduce the harms—social, legal, and otherwise—from their previous poor decision making—not just cynical assessments of the JDC.

Focusing on abstinence as the only definition of success further runs the risk of essentially having nothing to say to the sizable portion of juveniles who intend to resume smoking marijuana and drinking alcohol once they finish the program. Such a prevention strategy itself, then, may actually contribute to drug-related harm through its sheer irrelevance (J. Cohen, 1993, p. 68). A host of evaluative studies have shown that all kinds of primary prevention education programs and media campaigns, such as Drug Abuse Resistance Education (DARE), have failed to prevent or even reduce illicit drug use among young people (J. Cohen, 1993). Some studies indicate, moreover, that harm reduction messages are more positively received by users than abstinence; only education, and harm reduction can be a useful supplement to abstinence-based prevention that may alienate current or likely users (Hamilton, Cross, & Resnicow, 2000).

This is particularly salient for the JDC where the law is, as the judge explained it, black and white on the issue of certain drug taking, but life is not so black and white. Some professionals have indeed criticized the stringent laws for hindering primary prevention endeavors. Alexander and Wijngaart (1997) argue that, given the great variability of response to all drugs (legal and illegal), universal abstinence can only be advocated on a moral or religious, and not a therapeutic, basis (p. 82). The law's lumping together of all illicit drug use as "abuse," and the consequent refusal to recognize "recreational" or "responsible" use inhibits a productive discourse on the potential dangers, risks, and benefits presented by drugs in society.

* * *

There were benefits in the JDC. Youth reported controlling their drug use, getting along better with family, and improving in school. The question for juvenile drug courts is if the beneficial outcomes that do occur do so *in spite* of the labeling, punishment, and surveillance that comprise the chief components of treatment in the criminal justice system rather than because of them.

To date, it has been assumed that whatever success that is found in a drug court is directly related to surveillance and punishments. It might be, however, that many individuals operating within the program—both the youth and the staff—find meaning and success despite the coercive nature of the program and its fixation on drug test results and the proper ratio of carrots to sticks.

Success is found and nurtured within the fissures between these coercive components: a juvenile grew closer to his family, some took a step back from their drug use, another felt less angry, a juvenile appreciated the chance to talk and share with others in the group sessions, a counselor learned to interact with the youth with less confrontation.

It was not regular drug tests and increasing punishments that led to these successes. It was neither insisting a juvenile had a drinking problem because he once had a hangover, nor insisting another youth was a drug abuser destined for a life of the addiction disease. It was not family members turning each other into the police. It was not a carefully calibrated system of punishments. It was not detaining a kid with a shy bladder until he could pee in the cup. Drug court staff and proponents do a disservice to themselves and their clients when they assume it was.

Success occurred through conversation, openness to others' experiences, a true dialogue. It was when counselors were a little less "finger pointing" that they connected with the youths. It was in the car ride home that a father and son shared conversation. It was finding a new group of friends. It was getting their charges expunged, so they could leave the criminal justice system behind them.

Ultimately, the heart of the question revolves around whether the criminal justice system, with its tendency toward legalistic definitions of issues, labeling, coercion, obedience, surveillance, and the net-widening of state social control can even provide truly therapeutic benefits in a treatment milieu. To date, the literature, which presents drug courts as efficient models of compassionate coercion, is incomplete. In reality, individuals within the JDC have concerns, questions, and tensions that need to be further investigated so we can better understand how the therapeutic tools they use within a coercive environment help and hinder them from meeting their treatment goals.

In the interest of at least doing no further harm, it would seem that such attempts at coerced drug treatment should, at the very least, be reserved for the population for which it was intended, hardcore drug-addicted, recidivating offenders. To apply the same criteria and philosophies to juveniles arrested for marijuana possession and status offenses may risk doing more harm than good.

APPENDIX

I conducted this study while fulfilling a one-year contract as an evaluator for the JDC. Over the course of the year, I attended dozens of weekly compliance hearings in court, the prehearing staff meetings beforehand, and a few treatment meetings. During these observations, I chatted with staff and recorded notes.

I interviewed 25 juveniles, the judge, defender, prosecutor, 3 probation officers, and 6 treatment counselors. The juvenile interviews took place just before and sometimes during the court hearings. We met in a small room reserved for defense attorneys to meet with clients. It is connected to the large waiting room but provides ample privacy for the interviews. Interviews with the staff took place in or around their respective places of work. They typically lasted from half an hour to one hour each. One juvenile declined to be interviewed but did not give a reason. It seemed probable that he simply did not want to spend the time in an interview, since he was in Phase 2 and was waiting only to complete a drug test and leave. All interviews were tape-recorded and later transcribed.

In an attempt to include as much variation in experience as possible, I purposively selected the juvenile participants.[45] As I accumulated new insights and information while observing, working with, and talking to JDC staff and participants, I used sampling to refine my focus on individuals who seemed most relevant or difficult to reach (Lincoln & Guba, 1985). For instance, if I saw a youth get into trouble in court, I would approach the juvenile for an interview at the next hearing. If no other reason, the inherently shorter length of stay in the program for the expelled juveniles motivated me to talk with those who got in trouble as soon as possible to prevent an underrepresentation of these individuals. I also had to take extra efforts to get an overrepresentation of both females and African Americans, since they comprised a smaller portion of the JDC participants.

I tried to interview only juveniles who had spent at least two months in the program. This allowed for enough time in the program for the juvenile to gain a sense of it without allowing too much time to lose many of those who get expelled. Two of the juveniles, however, were interviewed just short of the two-month deadline.

Table 5 provides some descriptive information on the 25 juveniles I interviewed. The mean age is similar to the larger JDC population. Females were slightly overrepresented, and African Americans were underrepresented. I succeeded in getting more females but had trouble reaching African Americans. During my tenure with the court, it was difficult to identify eligible African Americans who had been in the program at least two months while I was conducting interviews. Although race did not significantly correlate with outcome, African American youths averaged over 3 weeks less in the program than Caucasians (20.6 weeks versus 23.8 weeks), reducing my chances of identifying an eligible participant.

More importantly, the average date for program admittance for African Americans was five months earlier than whites. In other words, there had been a substantial reduction in African American youth entering the program by the time I began my interviews. Some staff members had voiced concerns that a disproportionate number of African Americans were turning down JDC participation, opting for traditional adjudication. Since I began my interviews after this phenomenon had begun, my sample seems to underrepresent African Americans relative to the population for the first year. It was not, however, an underrepresentation relative to the population available at the time of the interviews.

Over the course of the study, 39 percent of the interviewees terminated from the program and 61 percent graduated. This rate is similar to that of the larger JDC population. Had the more problematic juveniles not been prioritized, they would likely have been underrepresented.

Table 5   Sample Characteristics

(N=25)

Age	15.7 (mean)
	16.0 (median)
Race	(%)
Caucasian	84.6
African American	15.4
Gender	(%)
Male	76.9
Female	23.1
Status	(%)
Completed	61.5
Expelled	38.5

Importantly, my sampling approach allowed flexibility in identifying potential interviewees in a dynamic program where a juvenile's program status could change quickly from hearing to hearing, based on a drug test result, a complaint from a parent, a problem in school, and more. Additionally, some youth were in for slightly less than or just a week or two past the two-month limit I used. Consequently, I could identify potential interviewees as I watched circumstances unfold in court and in the prehearing meetings.

In any event, interviews with these youths were conducted to the point of redundancy. That is, responses became increasingly repetitive to the point that I felt I had a solid cross-section of opinions and experiences. This redundancy is an important criterion for an exploratory study concerned with generating new hypotheses, and it is one for which purposive sampling is well suited (Lincoln & Guba, 1985). A different sampling frame would be more appropriate for a study that tested specific hypotheses.

I also had to decide the extent to which the interviews should be structured (or standardized). Broadly speaking, I faced three general options from which to choose: (1) allow each respondent to completely guide the conversation with little to no guidance from myself; (2) utilize an open-ended interview schedule with questions and probes; or (3) utilize a closed-ended structured interview instrument. The first option offers the promise of providing the richest data but also has the potential to miss information deemed important by the researcher. The third option allows for stringent tests of item reliability and validity, providing the standardization useful for comparisons between programs, but it risks silencing the participants' own concerns and interests (see Duffee & Duffee, 1981, for a discussion of the four options they considered).

So I decided on interviews with a set of open-ended questions and probes that would explore the participants' views and experiences while also ensuring that the issues of importance to me were covered at least in part. Though this compromised approach inhibits standardization and does not allow the subjects total freedom to share, it nonetheless balances the need for a certain richness of information with my interest in addressing some specific issues.

The very process of giving (an admittedly limited) voice to the juveniles under the supervision of the drug treatment court is in itself a bit of a departure from the traditional criminal justice's focus on the concerns of program managers and other stakeholders. Evaluations voicing the concerns of individuals (and groups of individuals) can give a moment of pause to programmatic policies that seek to apply universal treatments (Kushner, 2000, p. 11). They can be used to privilege individual voices over institutional voices and privilege the voices of those bound to receive program meanings over those who give the meanings of programs (Kushner, 2000, p. 41).

I also spoke with the JDC staff. While it is important to pay special attention to the marginalized voices of the young participants coerced into the program "for their own good," the voices of the people staffing the program—probation officers, treatment personnel, lawyers, and judge—must also be considered. Interviewing the "institutional voices" serves at least two purposes. First, though they certainly have relatively more power than the juveniles, their voices often tend to be subsumed by the needs and goals of other more powerful managers and policymakers, whose concerns take precedence. It is important to know the extent to which the drug court actors subscribe to the cases made on their behalf in the literature and the media. In practice, do they hold the same definitions of success as those described in the dominant discourse?

More importantly, staff views serve as points of contrast and comparison with the juveniles' definitions of success and experiences. They are the ones who punish juveniles for disobedience, reward them for compliance, and decide who is successful and who is not. For a more complete picture of how those involved experience the drug court, their views must be explored.

A study relying so heavily on interviews with individuals associated with a drug treatment program monitored by juvenile courts suffers some restrictions that can adversely affect the presentation of the information. Foremost, the interviews are a product of my interaction with the interviewees. They cannot be viewed as the autonomous products of each individual interviewed. How the participants related to me could greatly influence what they said, and what I offered back as well. Importantly, I did after all conduct the interviews while a contracted employee of the court. It often took a little time to get the juveniles to talk frankly outside of the program discourse. Some were reluctant to say anything beyond what they thought the program staff, me included, would want to hear. It was sometimes a challenge to overcome this, but it was, I think, usually overcome during an interview.

Sometimes, for example, a juvenile would talk about the benefits of giving up marijuana. Later in the interview, however, he would admit he had every intention of resuming his use of the drug as soon as he was out of the program. It often seemed the real barrier was the juveniles' view of me as an adult with similar expectations of deference and scripted responses. During one of my first interviews, a girl gave me a long speech on the joys of sobriety and the dangers of drugs. I walked away thinking what a great spokesperson she could be for the program, then a probation officer informed me she had been testing positive for marijuana and was getting into some trouble with the court. This problem became less difficult as I gained experience interviewing and the juvenile participants learned more about my role.

Others were pretty open up front, and still others undoubtedly were never so open. The number of juveniles who did indeed admit their intentions to at least consider future marijuana use and the enthusiasm with which some criticized the program and its personnel led me to believe that the majority were quite honest and did indeed feel comfortable in an interview taking place in a sometimes uncomfortable program. The book presents my own findings from these interviews and my observations. They are doubtless colored by my own many and multifaceted biases I brought to the project. Some of these biases changed significantly during my study, while others loosened just a bit. It is, I hope, an honest presentation of what I came to know.

NOTES

1 Though arrests and charges are not necessarily the same things, they do provide similar indicators of criminal justice involvement.

2 The number of drug offenders in the country's jails and prisons likewise skyrocketed. The percentage of jail inmates with drug offenses rose from 10 in 1983 to over 22 in 1989 (BJS, 1992). The number of drug offenders in federal prisons grew from 4,749 (25 percent) in 1980 to 27,310 (54 percent) in 1990 (BJS, 1992). In 1980, drug offenders comprised 25 percent, but by 1990 they made up more than 50 percent. The rate of incarceration in jails rose from 218 adult inmates per 100,000 residents in 1990 to 292 in 1998 (BJS, 2002). In 1998, 3.4 million adults were on probation (BJS, 2002). Of those, more than 470,000 were on probation for drug law violations. On June 20, 2006, 2,245,189 prisoners were held in federal or state prisons or in local jails.

3 Indeed, Francis Allen (1981) notes that almost all of the characteristic innovations in criminal justice of the twentieth century, including the juvenile court, the indeterminate sentence, systems of probation and parole, the youth authority, and the promise of therapeutic programs in prisons, juvenile institutions, and mental hospitals, are reflections of the rehabilitative ideal of turn-of-the-century Progressivism.

4 This state of affairs is hardly unique to drug treatment courts. In a metanalysis of 33 correction-based training programs for adult offenders, Wilson et al. (2000) found "A full 89 percent of the studies were judged to be of poor methodological quality. Thus, the generally positive findings may result from differential characteristics of the offenders rather than a positive effect of the program activities. That is, these groups could differ before program participation on important variables, such as degree of motivation to make positive life changes" (Wilson et al., 2000, pp. 361–362).

5 See Shaw and Robinson (1999) for a good example of this in a juvenile drug

court or see Holton (2003) for an example of skimming the experimental group and then not even including a control group for comparison.

6 Even some of these "more rigorous" studies, however, suffer sampling problems. Harrell and associates (2002), who are cited by Gottfredson, Najaka, and Kearley (2003) as an example of a rigorous study, completed an evaluation of a pretrial intervention program that included many drug court components, such as drug testing, supervision, collaboration, and drug treatment. The researchers compared 245 participants in the program with a sample of 137 defendants arrested prior to implementation of the program. The researchers found lower rates of drug use and recidivism among the intervention group. The preimplementation control group, however, had "significantly more prior criminal involvement (months incarcerated, prior arrests, probation or parole at the time of arrest), and had more employment problems than did the [experimental intervention group]" before entering the study (Harrell, Mitchell, Hirst, Marlowe, & Merrill, 2002, p. 197). Criminal history and employment history are two of the most powerful predictors of recidivism in criminological research. Thus, the control group was already at a much higher risk for "failure." The researchers, though, did attempt to statistically control for this difference.

7 In 2004, I published an op-ed in Join Together Online, criticizing the state of drug court research. Doug Marlowe (2004), a coauthor on one of the reports I had criticized for skimming, replied, "...the more studies that are conducted on an intervention, the greater is the probability that some of the studies will have been poorly implemented, the data poorly analyzed, or the implications overstated. This leaves proponents [of drug courts] open to the charge that they are relying on 'junk science'... However, there are at least three randomized controlled, experimental studies published in peer-reviewed journals reporting superior result for drug courts over traditional probationary conditions." The fact that the USGAO could identify only 27 out of 117 evaluations rigorous enough to include in their analysis seems to suggest that it is rather the reverse; there have been so many studies that finally a few have been found to have an effect. In fact, careful reading of the poorly designed research often finds no effects for the program, which is why the researchers ultimately skimmed, in order to show an effect where there was none. This is not to say that drug courts "don't work." But the argument that we can ignore a vast sea of bad studies all biased toward showing positive outcomes (when often there were none) because three good studies showed an effect seems tenuous at best. It is also important to bear in mind what I said in the text, that those studies Marlowe (2004) says "have been poorly implemented, the data poorly analyzed, or the implications overstated" have almost all erred on the side of showing drug court success. This suggests that the problem might be more than amateurish research design.

8 Ultimately, the most informative research will compare clients in coerced treatment not only with other treatment modalities, but also with similarly situated drug-using individuals not in treatment at all. This sort of research can best inform discussions of the harms and benefits of drugs versus the harms and benefits of coerced treatment or abstinence.

9 "The effect of coercing treatment for nondependent adolescents is unknown, but in many ways it violates the NIDA principles of effective treatment" (Rossman, Butts, Roman, DeStefano, & White, 2004, p. 97).

10 There are a few notable exceptions to this generalization. Applegate and Santana (2000), for example, explored the effects of juvenile drug court participation on the youths' social and psychological functioning. Initial scores on the Children's Global Assessment Scale were compared with scores at release. Overall, 57 percent of all discharged youths showed higher scores upon release, indicating higher levels of social and/or psychological functioning (Applegate & Santana, 2000). Of those released from the program, 42 percent successfully graduated and 58 percent were terminated unsuccessfully. Successful program graduates averaged a 17-point increase on the Children's Global Assessment Scale (CGAS), while those who failed actually decreased by 1.6 points.

An outcome evaluation of the Denver Adult DTC by Miethe and associates (2000), though concerned primarily with recidivism, did explore the possibly stigmatizing effects of certain drug court processes. When they found that drug court participants actually had higher recidivism rates than the control group, they attributed this to the stigmatizing nature of drug courts, which degrades participants when they enter but fails to maintain reintegrative efforts once they have graduated from the program. While in the program participants who failed to comply with the rules were, according to Miethe and associates (2000) often subjected to admonitions, berating, and labels of "drug addict" both in treatment and in court.

11 There is some concern that the anonymity of recovering members of AA may be threatened by the courts' requirement that defendants attain a signature from another AA member to prove that he or she attended a meeting. But anonymity in AA is meant to emphasize the notion that everyone is an equal part of a larger collective. One of the 12 Traditions of AA states, "Anonymity is the spiritual foundation of our Traditions, ever reminding us to place principles before personalities" (Pittman, 1988, p. 203). The importance of anonymity, then, lies not in the literal anonymity of members so much as in the spiritual lesson that no one is above anyone else.

12 This includes all the juveniles, but those in Phase 1 were tested more often, and those in Phase 2 were tested less often.

13 Although national "standard-setting" groups, such as the National Advisory Committee for Juvenile Justice and Delinquency Prevention and the National Advisory Committee on Criminal Justice Standards and Goals (1976), have recommended a 25-client caseload for all probation officers, very few probation departments are able to keep caseloads that low (Kurlychek, Torbet, & Bozynski, 1999).

14 It is not entirely clear what missing data in the assessment sheets resulted from the juvenile claiming no drug of choice and what resulted from assessments

incompletely filled out by the assessor. Sometimes, the assessment contained a notation specifically mentioning that no drug of choice was claimed by the juvenile; other times the spaces were simply left blank.

15 Material for Chapter 3 was reprinted from *International Journal of Drug Policy, 15(4),* K. Whiteacre, "Denial and Adversity in a Juvenile Drug Court," 279–304, (2004), with permission from Elsevier.

16 In observations of a traditional adult court, Mileski (1971) found that self-excusers, those who gave an account of their behavior in court, received harsher sentences than other defendants, even if they had already pled guilty. Interestingly, she attributes this to the fact that too much information from the defendant threatens the bureaucratic efficiency of the court system. Or as one juvenile complained, "... when you're actually in court, I just think they just want to get it over with, you know. They just want everybody to do it fast and stuff so everybody can go home. I know I want to get home as soon as I can."

17 An outcome evaluation of the Denver Adult DTC by Miethe and associates (2000) found that participants had *higher* recidivism rates than the control group. They attributed this to the stigmatizing nature of drug courts, which degrades participants when they enter but fails to maintain reintegrative efforts once they have graduated from the program. While in the program, participants who failed to comply with the rules were, according to Miethe et al., often subjected to admonitions, berating, and labels of "drug addict" both in treatment and in court.

18 Materials for Chapters 4 and 5 were reprinted from *Criminal Justice Policy Review, 18(3),* K. Whiteacre, "Strange Bedfellows: Tensions of Coerced Treatment," 260–273, (2007), with permission from SAGE.

19 Nolan (2001) has documented other euphemisms for punishment used by DTC personnel such as calling jail sanctions "shock therapy," "motivational jail," and "my motel" (p. 195). In another study, a DTC judge said he did not see enforcing sanctions as "imposing punishment but as providing help" (Satel, 1998, p. 52).

20 A telling illustration of this merging of orientations can be found in the argument made by the Director of National Affairs for the Drug Policy Alliance, the nation's largest organization for drug law reform, who writes without irony that "within the drug treatment court, 'sanctions' are not punishment. They are simply 'adjustments,' a device by which the court teaches addicts responsibility for their actions" (McColl, 2002, p. 19).

21 And there is a much longer Western tradition linking rehabilitation with punishment generally. Allen (1981) identifies the roots in the Old Testament. Aristotle spoke of punishment as "a kind of cure" (McColl, 2002, p. 13).

22 Maruna and LeBel (2003) note that in the United Kingdom, community service has simply been relabeled as a "community punishment order."

23 In fact, overnight detention was even considered by some of the staff as "no biggie."

24 Materials for Chapters 4 and 5 were reprinted from *Criminal Justice Policy Review, 18(3)*, K. Whiteacre, "Strange Bedfellows: Tensions of Coerced Treatment," 260–273, (2007), with permission from SAGE.

25 "But do not let us be deceived by a name. To be taken without consent from my home and friends; to lose my liberty; to undergo all those assaults on my personality which modern psychotherapy knows how to deliver; to be remade after some pattern of 'normality' hatched in a Viennese laboratory to which I never professed allegiance; to know that this process will never end until either my captors have succeeded or I grown wise enough to cheat them with apparent success—who cares whether this is called Punishment or not?" (Lewis, 1953, p. 227).

26 Similar criticisms have also been levied against the "Rehabilitative Ideal" by Frances Allen (1981) and many others. See Garland (2001, pp. 55–60) for a good discussion of some of the critiques of "Correctionalism" in America.

27 Others have suggested that it may violate certain notions of distributive justice to provide treatment to addicts who don't really want it (Farabee, Prendergast, & Anglin, 1998, p. 3).

28 The epigrammatic quote from the last chapter, "There's been a lot of kinks as to the focus... you know, whether it's more treatment-based or whether it's more punishment-based," illustrates the ambivalence among staff. The statement assumes that treatment and punishment are two competing ideas rather than the same components of a therapeutic program, this despite that the very basis of the program is the use of coercion for therapeutic goals.

29 No one, however, expressed concerns over civil liberties, autonomy, or tolerance.

30 See S. Cohen (1992) for a discussion of the "mystifying nature" of such "justificatory schemes" for more intrusive measures based on the evidence that they are as good as less intrusive measures.

31 Mileski (1971) notes, "From one perspective, defendants are as deviant if they do not conform to the routines of the court as they are if they do not conform to the rules of the state. Like the wider society it supports, the court has a social integrity which can be disrupted" (p. 473).

32 This provides a context for better understanding why disagreement is medicalized into "denial" and why denial, a symptom of a disease, is punished more harshly than confession, despite the doubts most staff had about the therapeutic value of punishment.

33 DuPont remains active proselytizing for drug testing of employees, individuals

with a driver's license and others and, coincidentally, heads the workplace drug testing consultation firm Bensinger, DuPont and Associates.

34 Sam Torres (1996) writes in *Federal Probation* that in most instances the collection process is actually far more unpleasant for the probation officer, who comes from a middle-class background, than for the offender "who has had the experience of losing his or her privacy while incarcerated" (p. 19).

> One need only recall a multiple-person jail cell with two, three, or even four bunks and a toilet in the middle of the cell... Many offenders have already experienced drug testing before probation or parole supervision. Many have been tested on pretrial supervision; others, who have been sentenced to some time in custody, already have been tested numerous times in an institution. Still others, however, who have had little or no experience of incarceration, may feel intense humiliation, embarrassment, and anger when observed urinating for a drug test. (Torres, 1996, p. 19)

35 It also ultimately works to normalize such increased surveillance in the wider society (Feeley & Simon, 1994).

36 Incidentally, next to it was another advertisement for "rapid on-site drug tests" produced by Roche Laboratories, developers of the extremely popular drug Valium, one of the more widely used drugs of choice among participants in adult drug courts.

37 In a study funded by the Substance Abuse Policy Research Program of the Robert Wood Johnson Foundation, researchers surveyed eight different Web sites for companies marketing drug detection kits to parents (Levy, Van Hook, & Knight, 2004). Five of the eight Web sites recommended repeated, random drug testing as the "mainstay" of a "family drug and alcohol policy" (Levy et al., 2004, p. 724). Though "[d]rug testing could be associated with unanticipated consequences such as a decrease in honest communication between parents and teens," three of the Web sites claimed that home drug testing would "open an honest conversation about drugs" (Levy et al., 2004, p. 725). Finally, the researchers concluded that "many of the claims of benefits of home drug testing made by the Web sites reviewed in this study are unsubstantiated," including claims that drug testing reduces use by reducing peer pressure or that drug tests provide a means for knowing for sure whether a child is using drugs or not (Levy et al., 2004, p. 726).

38 Some critics have, in fact, argued that today's Information Age might be better described as the Surveillance Age (Flaherty, 1988). The same AMA (2001b) survey, which found that 67 percent of companies drug test employees, also found that "[m]ore than three-quarters (77.7%) of major U.S. firms record and review employee communications and activities on the job, including their phone calls,

e-mail, Internet connections, and computer files. The figure has doubled since 1997, when AMA inaugurated its annual survey."

39 Of course, use of anonymous informants is not restricted to schools. Thousands of anonymous hot lines are used in the United States by police agencies and private employers in the drug war. Rosenbaum (1998) writes, "While the provision of anonymity allows informants to report illegal drug activity without fear of retaliation, it has also opened the door to potential abuses of this privilege and to false reporting of information about neighbors, acquaintances, lovers, competitors, and others without sanction... Again, citizens have shown a strong willingness to participate as informants in these programs without reservation" (p. 212).

40 This recidivism rate was about the same as a comparison group made up of similarly situated juveniles who opted out of the program.

41 Thirty years ago, Wexler (1972), a proponent of therapeutic justice, warned that the greatest threat from the approach was its potential to be limitless.

> Of the multitude of problems associated with the therapeutic model, the great bulk can be summarized under a single unifying theme: that the therapeutic approach knows no bounds. If through the use of modern scientific techniques, the prevention or cure of deviant behavior is elevated to a superseding status, all other factors that have long been traditionally embedded in our jurisprudence are definition dwarfed. (Wexler, 1972, p. 293)

42 Incidentally, these recommendations are similar in spirit to Pepinsky's (2006) four procedural safeguards to ensure that state support services do not become equivalent to state supervision: (1) there should be no conditions on the individual asking for help; (2) there should be no conditions on how contact will be maintained; (3) the state should not maintain additional records of information (or dossiers) on the individual not already available publicly; and (4) the state will not initiate legal actions against the individual coming for services.

43 For some critics, holding people responsible to authority only perpetuates existing power imbalances and may even make the people involved less safe (Pepinsky, 1998). It perpetuates its own false justification—that power holders always know better than subordinates. In fact *holding* someone responsible is, for Pepinsky (1998), a contradiction in terms.

44 Of course, addicted alcoholics (rather than problem drinkers) usually cannot go back to moderate drinking. But this is not of much relevance to the JDC clientele.

45 Lincoln and Guba (1985, pp. 201–202) list several characteristics of purposive sampling consistent with the design and aims of this research project.

BIBLIOGRAPHY

AITQ. (1995). *Strategies de reduction des mefaits en matiere de drogues qui s'inscrivent dans une politique globale de promotion de la sante*. Montreal: Association des Intervenants en Toxicomanies du Quebec.

Ackerman, D. L. (1991). A history of drug testing. In Coombs, R. H. & West, L. J. (Eds.), *Drug testing: Issues and options* (pp. 3–21). New York: Oxford University Press.

Ainsworth, J. E. (1991). Re-imagining childhood and deconstructing the legal order: The case for abolishing the juvenile court. *North Carolina Law Review, 69*, 1083–1132.

Alexander, B. K. & Van de Wijngaart, G. F. (1997). Readiness for harm reduction: Coming to grips with the temperance mentality. In Erickson, P. G., Riley, D. M., Chueng, Y. W., & O'Hare, P. (Eds.), *Harm reduction: A new direction for drug policies and programs* (pp. 80–98). Toronto: Toronto University Press.

Allen, F. A. (1981). *The decline of the rehabilitative ideal*. New Haven, CT: Yale University Press.

American Academy of Child & Adolescent Psychiatry. (2004a). *Children who can't pay attention/ADHD*. Retrieved on September 9, 2007, from http://www.aacap.org/cs/root/facts_for_families/children_who_cant_pay_attention/adhd.

———. (2004b). *Children with oppositional defiant disorder*. Retrieved on September 9, 2007, from http://www.aacap.org/cs/root/facts_for_families/children_with_oppositional_defiant_disorder.

American Friends Service Committee (AFSC). (1971). *Struggle for justice.* New York: Hill & Wang.

American Management Association (AMA). (2001a). *2001 AMA survey on workplace testing: Medical Testing.* New York: American Management Association.

————. (2001b). *2001 AMA survey: Workplace monitoring & surveillance.* New York: American Management Association.

Anderson, E., Levine, M., Sharma, A., Ferretti, L., Steinberg, K., & Wallach, L. (1993). Coercive use of mandatory reporting in therapeutic relationships. *Behavioral Sciences and the Law, 11*(3), 335–345.

Anglin, M. D. & Hser, Y. (1990). Treatment of drug abuse. In Tonry, M. & Wilson, J. Q. (Eds.), *Drugs and crime* (pp. 393–460). Chicago: University of Chicago Press.

Applegate, B. K. & Santana, S. (2000). Intervening with youthful substance abusers: A preliminary analysis of a juvenile drug court. *Justice System, 21*(3), 281–300.

Baekeland, F., L. Lundwall, and B. Kissin. (1975). Methods for the Treatment of Chronic Alcoholism: A Critical Appraisal. In Gibbons, R. J., Y. Israel, H. Kalant, R.E. Popham, W. Schmidt, and R. G. Smart (Eds). *Research Advances in Alcohol and Drug Problems,* Vol. 2, ed. New York: Wiley.

Beauchesne, L. (1997). Legalization of drugs: Responsible action towards health promotion and effective harm reduction strategies. In Erickson, P. G., Riley, D. M., Chueng, Y. W., & O'Hare, P. (Eds.), *Harm reduction: A new direction for drug policies and programs* (pp. 32–46). Toronto: Toronto University Press.

Belenko, S. (1998). Research on drug courts: A critical review. *National Drug Court Institute Review, 1*(1), 1–42.

————. (1999). Research on drug courts: A critical review (1999 update). *National Drug Court Institute Review, 2*(2), 1–58.

————. (2001). *Research on drug courts: A critical review* (2001 update). The National Center on Addiction and Substance Abuse at Columbia University.

Boldt, R. C. (1998). Rehabilitative punishment and the drug treatment court movement. *Washington University Law Quarterly, 76,* 1205–1306.

————. (2002). The adversary system and attorney role in the drug treatment court movement. In Nolan, J. L. (Ed.), *Drug courts in theory and in practice* (pp. 115–143). New York: Aldine de Gruyter.

Braithwaite, J. (1999). *Crime, shame and reintegration.* Cambridge: Cambridge University Press.

Bureau of Justice Assistance (BJA). (2000). *Drug use, testing, and treatment in jails.* Washington, DC: U.S. Department of Justice.

Bureau of Justice Assistance Drug Court Clearinghouse. (2006, June 15). *Drug court activity update.* Washington, DC: American University.

Bureau of Justice Statistics (BJS). (1992). *Treatment alternatives to street crime: TASC programs.* Washington, DC: U.S. Department of Justice.

―――. (2002). *Correctional populations in the United States— Statistical tables.* Retrieved on June 1, 2007, from http://www.ojp.usdoj.gov/bjs/abstract/cpusst.htm.

―――. (2007a). *Drug law violations.* Retrieved on March 25, 2007, from http://www.ojp.usdoj.gov/bjs/dcf/tables/arrtot.htm.

―――. (2007b). *Drugs and crime facts.* Retrieved on March 25, 2007, from http://www.ojp.usdoj.gov/bjs/dcf/enforce.htm.

Butts, J. A. & Roman, J. (2004). Drug courts in the juvenile justice system. In Butts, J. A. & Roman, J. (Eds.), *Juvenile drug courts and teen substance abuse* (pp. 1–25). Washington, Roman, J. & DeStefano, C. (2004). Drug court effects and the quality of existing evidence. In DC: Urban Institute.

Cohen, J. (1993). Achieving a reduction in drug-related harm through education. In Heather, N., Wodak, A., Nadelmann, E. A., & O'Hare, P. (Eds.), Psychoactive drugs and harm reduction: From faith to science (pp. 65–76). London: Whurr Publishers.

Cohen, S. (1992). *Against criminology.* New Brunswick, NJ: Transaction Publishers.

Cooper, C. S. & Bartlett, S. (1998). *Juvenile and family drug courts: Profile of program characteristics and implementation issues.* Drug Court Clearinghouse and Technical Assistance Project. Washington, DC: American University.

Cooper, C. S. & Trotter, J. A. (1994). Recent developments in drug case management: Re-engineering the judicial process. *The Justice System Journal, 17*(1), 1–17.

Cosden, M., Basch, J. E., Campos, E., Greenwell, A., Barazani, S., & Walker, S. (2006). Effects of motivation and problem severity on court-based drug treatment. *Crime & Delinquency, 52*(4), 599–618.

Curtis, R. (2002). Quality of life obsessions and the micro-management of behavior. *Criminology and Public Policy, 1*(2), 245–250.

Deci, E. L. & Ryan, R. M. (1985). Intrinsic motivation and self-determination in human behavior. New York: Plenum Press.

De Leon, G. (1988). Legal pressure in therapeutic communities. In Leukfeld, C. G. & Tims, F. M. (Eds.), *Compulsory treatment of drug abuse: Research and clinical practice*, NIDA Research Monograph 86, Rockville, MD: National Institute on Drug Abuse.

Denning, P. (2000). *Practicing harm reduction psychotherapy.* New York: Guilford Press.

De Rios, M. D. & Smith, D. E. (1977). Drug use and abuse in cross cultural perspective. *Human Organization, 36*(1), 14–21.

Deschenes, E. P. & Greenwood, P. W. (1994). *Maricopa County's drug court: An innovative program for first time offenders on probation.* California: RAND.

Duffee, D. E. & Duffee, B. W. (1981). Studying the needs of offenders in prerelease centers. *Journal of Research in Crime and Delinquency, 18*(2), 232–253.

Duncan, D. F. (1992). Drug abuse prevention in post-legalization America: What could it be like? *The Journal of Primary Prevention, 12*(4), 317–322.

Enzle, M. E. & Anderson, S. C. (1993). Surveillant intentions and intrinsic motivation. *Journal of Personality and Social Psychology, 64*(2), 257–266.

Farabee, D., Prendergast, M., & Anglin, M. D. (1998). The effectiveness of coerced treatment for drug-abusing offenders. *Federal Probation, 62*, 3–10.

Federal Bureau of Investigation (FBI). (1995). *Uniform crime reports.* Retrieved on June 7, 2007, from http://www.fbi.gov/ucr/95cius.htm.

Feeley, M. & Simon, J. (1994). Actuarial justice: The emerging new criminal law. In Nelken, D. (Ed.), *The future of criminology* (pp. 449–474). Thousand Oaks, CA: Sage Publications.

Feld, B. C. (1993). Criminalizing the American juvenile court. In Tonry, M. (Ed.), *Crime and justice: A review of research* (Vol. 17) (pp. 197–279). Chicago: University of Chicago Press.

Flaherty, D. H. (1988). The emergence of surveillance societies in the Western world: Toward the year 2000. *Government Information Quarterly, 5*(4), 377–387.

Fluellen, R. & Trone, J. (2000). *Do drug courts save jail and prison beds?* New York: Vera Institute of Justice.

Foucault, M. (1995 [1977]). *Discipline and punish: The birth of the prison.* New York: Vintage Books.

Friedman, A. S., Granick, S., & Kreisher, C. (1994). Motivation of adolescent drug abusers for help and treatment. *Journal of Child and Adolescent Substance Abuse, 3*(1), 69–88.

Furedi, F. (2002). Drug control and the ascendancy of Britain's therapeutic culture. In Nolan, J. L. (Ed.), *Drug courts in theory and in practice* (pp. 215–233). New York: Aldine de Gruyter.

Garland, D. (1990). *Punishment and modern society.* Chicago: University of Chicago Press.

———. (2001). *The culture of control.* Chicago: University of Chicago Press.

Gilliom, J. (1994). *Surveillance, privacy, and the law.* Ann Arbor: University of Michigan Press.

Goerdt, J. & Martin, J. A. (1989). The impact of drug cases on case processing in urban trial courts. *State Court Journal, 13*(4), 4–12.

Goldkamp, J. S. (1993). *Justice and treatment innovation: The drug court movement.* A working paper for the first National Drug Court Conference. Washington, DC: National Institute of Justice.

———. (1994). Miami's treatment drug court for felony defendants: Some implications for assessment findings. *The Prison Journal, 73*(2), 110–166.

Goldkamp, J. S. & Weiland, D. (1993). *Assessing the impact of Dade County's Felony Drug Court.* Philadelphia: Crime and Justice Research Institute.

Goldkamp, J. S., White, M. D., & Robinson, J. B. (2001). Do drug courts work? Getting inside: The drug court black box. *Journal of Drug Issues, 31*, 27–72.

Gottfredson, D. C., Najaka, S. S., & Kearley, B. (2003). Effectiveness of drug treatment courts: Evidence from a randomized trial. *Criminology & Public Policy, 2*(2), 171–196.

Haapanen, R. & Britton, L. (2002). Drug testing for youthful offenders on parole: An experimental evaluation. *Criminology and Public Policy, 1*(2), 217–244.

Hamilton, G., Cross, D., & Resnicow, K. (2000). Occasional cigarette smokers: Cue for harm reduction smoking education. *Addiction Research, 8*(5), 419.

Harford, R. J., Ungerer, J. C., & Kinsella, J. K. (1976). Effects of legal pressure on prognosis for treatment of drug dependence. *American Journal of Psychiatry, 133*(12), 1399–1403.

Harrell, A., Cavanagh, S., & Roman, J. (1998). Final report: Findings from the evaluation of the D.C. Superior Court Drug Intervention Program. Washington, DC: Urban Institute.

Harrell, A., Mitchell, O., Hirst, A., Marlowe, D., & Merrill, J. (2002). Breaking the cycle of drugs and crime: Findings from the Birmingham BTC demonstration. *Criminology & Public Policy, 1*(2), 189–216.

Harris, M. K. (1991). Moving into the new millennium: Toward a feminist vision of justice. In Pepinsky, H. E. & Quinney, R. (Eds.), *Criminology as peacemaking* (pp. 83–97). Bloomington: Indiana University Press.

Hoffman, A. (1987). *Steal this urine test*. New York: Penguin Books.

Hoffman, M. B. (2000). The drug court scandal. *North Carolina Law Review, 78*, 1437.

———. (2002). The Denver Drug Court and its unintended consequences. In Nolan, J. L. (Ed.), *Drug courts in theory and in practice* (pp. 67–88). New York: Aldine de Gruyter.

Holton, L. (2003). *New report shows drug courts are cost-effective, help rebuild lives*. News Release, April 15, Judicial Council of California, Administrative Office of the Courts.

Hora, P. F., Schma, W. G., & Rosenthal, J. T. A. (1999). Therapeutic jurisprudence and the drug treatment court movement: Revolutionizing the criminal justice system's response to drug abuse and crime in America. *Notre Dame Law Review, 74*, 439–538.

Hubbard, R. L., Collins, J. J., Rachal, J. V., & Cavanaugh, E. R. (1988). The criminal justice client in drug abuse treatment. In

Leukfeld, C. G. & Tims, F. M. (Eds.), *Compulsory treatment of drug abuse: Research and clinical practice*, NIDA Research Monograph 86. Rockville, MD: National Institute on Drug Abuse.

Huddleston, C. W., Freeman-Wilson, K., Marlowe, D. B., & Roussell, A. (2005). *Painting the current picture: A national report card on drug courts and other problem solving court programs in the United States, 1*(2). Bureau of Justice Assistance, Office of Justice Programs. Washington, DC: U.S. Department of Justice.

Hutchens, N. H. (2002). Suspicionless drug testing: The tuition for attending public school? *Alabama Law Review, 53,* 1265.

International Harm Reduction Association. (2007). *What is harm reduction?* Retrieved on April 26, 2007, from http://www.ihra.net/whatisharmreduction.

Join Together Online. (2003a). Sales of home drug-test kits on the rise. *News Summary.* Retrieved on May 9, 2003, from http://www.jointogether.org.

————. (2003b). Study: School drug testing doesn't deter drug use. *News Summary.* Retrieved on May 19, 2003, from http://www.jointogether.org.

Karoly, P. (1980). Person variables in therapeutic change and development. In Karoly, P. & Steffen, J. J. (Eds.), *Improving the long-term effects of psychotherapy* (pp. 195–261). New York: Gardner.

Kishline, A. (1994). *Moderate drinking.* New York: Three Rivers Press.

Kleiman, M. A. R. (1992). *Against excess: Drug policy for results.* New York: Basic Books.

Kurlychek, M., Torbet, P., & Bozynski, M. (1999). Focus on accountability: Best practices for juvenile court and probation. *JAIBG Bulletin,* September, U.S. Department of Justice, Office of Justice Programs, Office of Juvenile Justice and Delinquency Prevention.

Kushner, S. (2000). *Personalizing evaluation.* London: Sage Publications.

Latessa, E. J., Listwan, S. J., Shaffer, D. K., Lowenkamp, C., & Ratansi, S. (2001). *Preliminary evaluation of Ohio's drug court efforts.* Cincinnati, OH: Center for Criminal Justice Research, Division of Criminal Justice, University of Cincinnati.

Latessa, E. J., Shaffer, D. K., & Lowenkamp, C. (2002). *Outcome evaluation of Ohio's drug court efforts.* Cincinnati, OH: Center for Criminal Justice Research, Division of Criminal Justice, University of Cincinnati.

Lepper, M. R. & Greene, G. (1975). Turning play into work: Effects of adult surveillance and extrinsic rewards on children's intrinsic motivation. *Journal of Personality and Social Psychology, 31,* 479–486.

Leukfeld, C. G. & Tims, F. T. (Eds.). (1988). Compulsory treatment: A review of findings. *Compulsory treatment of drug abuse: Research and clinical practice,* NIDA Research Monograph 86, Rockville, MD: National Institute on Drug Abuse.

Levy, S., Van Hook, S., & Knight, J. (2004). A review of Internet-based home drug-testing products for parents. *Pediatrics, 113,* 720–726.

Lewis, C. S. (1953). The humanitarian theory of punishment. *Res Judicatae, 6,* 224–230.

Lincoln, Y. S. & Guba, E. G. (1985). *Naturalistic inquiry.* Beverly Hills, CA: Sage Publications.

Lipscher, R. D. (1989). The judicial response to the drug crisis, a report of an executive symposium involving judicial leaders of the nation's nine most populous states. *State Court Journal, 13*(4), 13–17.

Marlowe, D. B. (2004). *Drug court efficacy vs. effectiveness.* Retrieved on September 29, 2004, from http://www.jointogether.org.

Marlowe, D. B. & Kirby, K. C. (1999). Effective use of sanctions in drug courts: Lessons from behavioral research. *National Drug Court Institute Review, 2,* 1–32.

Martinson, R. (1974). What works? Questions and answers about prison reform. *The Public Interest, 35,* 22–54.

Maruna, S. & LeBel, T. P. (2003). Welcome home? Examining the "reentry court" concepts from a strengths-based perspective. *Western Criminology Review, 4*(2), 91–107.

McColl, W. D. (1996). Baltimore city's drug treatment court: Theory and practice in an emerging field. *Maryland Law Review, 55,* 467–518.

————. (2002). Theory and practice in the Baltimore city drug treatment court. In Nolan, J. L. (Ed.), *Drug courts in theory and in practice* (pp. 3–26). New York: Aldine de Gruyter.

Mears, D. P. (2004). Identifying adolescent substance abuse. In Butts, J. A. & Roman, J. (Eds.), *Juvenile drug courts and teen substance abuse* (pp. 185–220). Washington, DC: Urban Institute.

Miethe, T. D., Lu, H., & Reese, E. (2000). Reintegrative shaming and recidivism risks in drug court: Explanations for some unexpected findings. *Crime & Delinquency, 46*(4), 522–541.

Mileski, M. (1971). Courtroom encounters. *Law and Society Review, 5*(4), 473–538.

Miller, A. (1994). *The drama of the gifted child.* New York: Basic Books.

Miller, W. R. (1985). Motivation for treatment: A review with special emphasis on alcoholism. *Psychological Bulletin, 98,* 84–117.

———. (1991). Emergent treatment concepts and techniques. *Annual Review of Addictions Research and Treatment, 2,* 283–296.

Morris, N. & Buckle, D. (1953). The humanitarian theory of punishment: A reply. *Res Judicatae, 6,* 231–237.

Mumola, C. J. (1998). *Substance abuse and treatment of adults on probation, 1995.* U.S. Department of Justice. Washington, DC: Bureau of Justice Statistics.

National Advisory Committee on Criminal Justice Standards and Goals (1976). *Juvenile justice and delinquency prevention: Report of the Task Force on Juvenile Justice and Delinquency Prevention.* Washington, DC: U.S. Government Printing Office.

National Association of Drug Court Professionals (1997). *Defining drug courts: The key components.* Drug Courts Program Office, Office of Justice Programs. Washington, DC: U.S. Department of Justice.

National Association of Drug Court Professionals and The Office of Community Oriented Policing Services. (1998). *Community policing and drug courts/community courts: Working together within a unified court system.* Washington, DC: U.S. Department of Justice.

National Institute of Justice. (2003, April). *2000 Arrestee drug abuse monitoring: Annual report.* Retrieved on May 25, 2007, from http://www.ncjrs.gov/txtfiles1/nij/193013.txt.

Nolan, J. L., Jr. (2001). *Reinventing justice: The American drug court movement.* Princeton: Princeton University Press.

————. (Ed.). (2002). Separated by an uncommon law: Drug courts in Great Britain and America. *Drug courts in theory and in practice.* New York: Aldine de Gruyter.

NPC Research. (2006). *Hartford county juvenile drug court performance evaluation: Final report.* Retrieved on June 1, 2007, from http://spa.american.edu/justice/documents/58.pdf.

Office of Justice Programs (OJP). (January 2001). *Juvenile Drug Court Activity Update.* Washington, DC: OJP Drug Court Clearinghouse and Technical Assistance Project, American University.

Office of Juvenile Justice and Delinquency Program. (2007a). *Overview of the JABG program.* Retrieved on March 15, 2007, from http://ojjdp.ncjrs.org.

————. (2007b). *Purpose areas.* Retrieved on March 15, 2007, from http://ojjdp.ncjrs.org/jabg/purpose.html.

Office of National Drug Control Policy (ONDCP). (2002). *National drug control strategy.* Washington, DC: U.S. Government Printing Office.

Peele, S. & Brodsky, A. (2001). Gateway to nowhere: How alcohol came to be scapegoated for drug abuse. In Inciardi, J. A. & McElrath, K. (Eds.), *The American drug scene* (pp. 58–63). Los Angeles: Roxbury Publishing.

Pepinsky, H. (1995). Peacemaking primer. *Peace and Conflict Studies, 2,* 231–252.

————. (1998). Empathy works, obedience doesn't. *Criminal Justice Policy Review, 9*(2), 141–167.

————. (2006). *Peacemaking: Reflections of a radical criminologist.* Ontario: University of Ottawa Press.

Petersilia, J. (2003). *When prisoners come home.* New York: Oxford University Press.

Pittman, B. (1988). *AA: The way it began.* Seattle, WA: Glen Abbey Books.

Platt, A. M. (1977). *The child savers: The invention of delinquency.* Chicago: University of Chicago Press.

Potter, B. A. & Orfali, J. S. (1995). *Pass the test: An employee guide to drug testing.* Berkeley, CA: RONIN Publishing.

Prochaska, J. O. & DiClemente, C. C. (1992). Stages of change in the modification of problem behaviors. In Hersen, M., Eisler R. M., & Miller P. M. (eds.). *Progress in behavior modification* (pp. 184–214). Sycamore, IL: Sycamore Press.

Prochaska, J. O., DiClemente, C. C., & Norcross, J. C. (1992). In search of how people change. *American Psychologist, 47*(9), 1102–1114.

Quinn, M. C. (2000). Whose team am I on anyway? Musings of a public defender about drug treatment court practice. *New York University Review of Law and Social Change, 26*, 37.

Rinaldi, R. C., Steindler, E. M., Wilford, B. B., & Goodwin, D. (1988). Clarification and standardization of substance abuse terminology. *JAMA, 259*(4), 555–557.

Roan, S. (2007). Put to the test. *Los Angeles Times*, May 21.

Roman, J. & DeStefano, C. (2004). Drug court effects and the quality of existing evidence. In Butts, J. A. & Roman, J. (Eds.), *Juvenile drug courts and teen substance abuse* (pp. 107–135). Washington, DC: Urban Institute.

Roman, J. & Harrell, A. (2001). Assessing the costs and benefits accruing to the public from a graduated sanctions program for drug-using defendants. *Law and Policy, 23*(2), 237–268.

Roman, J., Butts, J. A., & Rebeck, A. S. (2004). American drug policy and the evolution of drug treatment courts. In Butts, J. A. & Roman, J. (Eds.), *Juvenile drug courts and teen substance abuse* (pp. 27–54). Washington, DC: Urban Institute.

Rosenberg, C. M. & Liftik, J. (1976). Use of coercion in the outpatient treatment of alcoholism. *Journal of Studies on Alcohol, 37*(1), 58–65.

Rossman, S. B., Butts, J. A., Roman, J. DeStefano, C., & White, R. (2004). What juvenile drug courts do and how they do it. In Butts, J. A. & Roman, J. (Eds.), *Juvenile drug courts and teen substance abuse* (pp. 55–106). Washington, DC: Urban Institute.

Sanford, J. S. & Arrigo, B. A. (2005). Lifting the cover on drug courts: Evaluation findings and policy concerns. *International Journal of Offender Therapy and Comparative Criminology, 49*(3), 239–259.

Satel, S. L. (1998). Observational study of courtroom dynamics in selected drug courts. *National Drug Court Institute Review, 1*(1), 43–72.

Schwebel, R. (2002, February). Drug courts and adolescents. *Counselor*, 14–19.

SCRAM (2007). *Products*. Retrieved on May 21, 2007, from http://www.alcoholmonitoring.com/products/index.html.

Shaw, M. & Robinson, K. D. (1999). Research update: Reports on recent drug court research. *National Drug Court Institute Review*, *2*(2), 135–150.

Shuman, D. W. (1996). The duty of the state to rescue the vulnerable in the United States. In Wexler, D. B. & Winick, B. J. (Eds.), *Law in a Therapeutic Key* (pp. 299–322). Durham, NC: Carolina Academic Press.

Smith, K. J., Subich, L. M., & Kalodner, C. (1995). The transtheoretical model's stages and processes of change and their relation to premature termination. *Journal of Counseling Psychology*, *42*, 34–39.

Stahler, G. J., Cohen, E., Greene, M. A., Shipley, T. E., & Bartelt, D. (1995). A qualitative study of treatment success among homeless crack-addicted men: Definitions and attributions. *Contemporary Drug Problems*, *22*(2), 237–264.

Tauber, J. S. (1993). *A judicial primer on unified drug courts and court-ordered drug rehabilitation programs.* Presented at the California Continuing Studies Program Dana Point. California, August 20.

———. (1994). Drug courts: A judicial manual. *CJER Journal*, California Center for Judicial and Education Research, Summer.

Taxman, F. S. & Bouffard, J. A. (2005). Treatment as part of drug court: The impact on graduation rates. *Journal of Offender Rehabilitation*, *42*(1), 23–50.

Torres, S. (1996). The use of a credible drug testing program for accountability and intervention. *Federal Probation*, *60*(4), 18–23.

———. (2000). Selecting the substance abuse specialist. *Federal Probation*, *64*(1), 46–50.

Turner, S., Petersilia, J., & Deschenes, E. (1992). Evaluating intensive supervision probation/parole (ISP) for drug offenders. *Crime and Delinquency*, *38*(4), 539–556.

Turner, S., Greenwood, P., Fain, T., & Deschenes, E. (1999). Perceptions of drug court: How offenders view ease of program completion, strengths and weaknesses, and the impact on their lives. *National Drug Court Review*, *2*(1), 61–86.

Wishnia, S. (2002). No rights for students. *High Times*, October.

United Nations. (1992). *The United Nations and drug abuse control.* United Nations International Drug Control Programme.

United States General Accounting Office (USGAO). (1995). *Drug courts: Information on a new approach to address drug-related crime*, Briefing Report to the Committee on the Judiciary, U.S. Senate, and the Committee on the Judiciary, House of Representatives, May.

———. (1997). *Drug courts: Overview of growth, characteristics, and results*. Report to the Committee on the Judiciary, U.S. Senate, and the Committee on the Judiciary, House of Representatives, July.

———. (2002). *Drug courts: Better DOJ data collection and evaluation efforts needed to measure impact of drug court programs*. Report to Congressional Requesters, April.

United States Government Accountability Office (USGAO). (2005). *Adult drug courts: Evidence indicates recidivism reductions and mixed results from other outcomes*. Report to Congressional Committees. Retrieved on June 1, 2007, from http://www.gao.gov/new.items/d05219.pdf.

Vaillant, George E. (1983). *The Natural History of Alcoholism*. Cambridge, MA: Harvard University Press.

Volpicelli, J. & Szalavitz, M. (2000). *Recovery options: The complete guide*. New York: John Wiley & Sons.

Walsh, J. M. & Trumble, J. G. (1991). The politics of drug testing. In Coombs, R. H. & West, L. J. (Eds.), *Drug testing: Issues and options* (pp. 22–49). New York: Oxford University Press.

Washington State Institute for Public Policy. (2003). Washington state's drug courts for adult defendants: Outcome evaluation and cost-benefit analysis. Olympia, WA.

Weil, A. & Rosen, W. (1998). *From chocolate to morphine*. Boston: Houghton Mifflin Company.

Wexler, D. B. (1972). Therapeutic justice. *Minnesota Law Review, 57*, 289.

Wexler, D. B. & Winick, B. J. (1991). Therapeutic jurisprudence as a new approach to mental health law policy analysis and research. *University of Miami Law Review, 45*(5), 979–1004.

White, G. E. (1972). From sociological jurisprudence to realism: Jurisprudence and social change in early twentieth-century America. *Virginia Law Review, 58*, 999–1028.

White, R. K. (1998). Family intervention: Background, principles, and other strategies. In White, R. K. & Wright, D. G. (Eds.),

Addiction intervention: Strategies to motivate treatment-seeking behavior (pp.7–20). New York: Haworth Press.

Whiteacre, K. (2004). Criminal constructions of drug users. In Palacios, W. (Ed.), *Cocktails and dreams: An interpretive perspective* (pp. 3–13). Upper Saddle River, NJ: Prentice-Hall.

Whiteacre, K. (2004). "Denial and Adversity in a Juvenile Drug Court." *International Journal of Drug Policy, 15(4)*, 279–304.

Whiteacre, K. (2007). "Strange Bedfellows: Tensions of Coerced Treatment." *Criminal Justice Policy Review, 18(3)*, 260–273.

Whiteacre, K. & Pepinsky, H. (2002). Controlling drug use. *Criminal Justice Policy Review, 13*(1), 21–31.

Wilson, D. J. (2000). *Drug use, testing, and treatment in jails.* U.S. Department of Justice, Bureau of Justice Statistics, Washington, DC: U.S. Government Printing Office.

Wilson, D. B., Gallagher, C. A., & MacKenzie, D. L. (2000). A meta-analysis of corrections-based education, vocation, and work programs for adult offenders. *Journal of Research in Crime and Delinquency, 37*(4), 347–368.

Winick, B. J. (1997). (Ed.), *Therapeutic jurisprudence applied: Essays on mental health law.* Durham, NC: Carolina Academic Press.

Wish, E. D. & Gropper, B. A. (1990). Drug testing by the criminal justice system. In Tonry, M. & Wilson, J. Q. (Eds.), *Drugs and crime* (pp. 321–391). Chicago: University of Chicago Press.

World Health Organization. (1998). *Health promotion glossary.* Switzerland: Division of Health Promotion, Education, and Communications.

Yamaguchi, R., Johnston, L. D., & O'Malley, P. M. (2003). Relationship between student illicit drug use and school drug-testing policies. *Journal of School Health, 73*(4), 159–164.l.

Court Cases

Board of Education of Independent School District No. 92 of Pottawatomie County et al., *Petitioners v. Lindsay Earls* et al., 122 S. Ct. 2559 (2002).

Skinner v. Railway Labor Executives' Association, 839 F. 2d 575 (1989).

Veronia School District 47J v. Wayne Acton, 515 U.S. 646 (1995).

NEW PERSPECTIVES
IN CRIMINOLOGY
AND CRIMINAL JUSTICE

Jeffrey Ian Ross, *General Editor*

This book series is a forum for cutting-edge work that pushes the boundaries of the disciplines of criminology and criminal justice, with the aim of exploring eclectic, un- and under-explored issues, and imaginative approaches in terms of theory and methods. Although primarily designed for criminology and criminal justice audiences—including scholars, instructors, and students—books in the series function across disciplines, appealing to those with an interest in anthropology, cultural studies, sociology, political science, and law.

Books in the series include:

Hawking Hits on the Information Highway, by Laura Finley
Blood, Power and Bedlam: State Crimes and Crimes Against Humanity in Post-Colonial Africa, by Christopher W. Mullins and Dawn L. Rothe
Chinese Policing: History and Reform, by Kam C. Wong
Arrest Decisions: What Works for the Officer? by Edith Linn
Drug Court Justice: Experiences in a Juvenile Drug Court, by Kevin Whiteacre

Authors who would like to submit a proposal for a volume in the series, or a completed book manuscript please direct all inquiries to:

Chris Myers, Peter Lang Publishing, 29 Broadway, New York, NY, 10006
ChrisM@plang.com

To order other books in this series, please contact our Customer Service Department:

800-770-LANG (within the U.S.)
212-647-7706 (outside the U.S.)
212-647-7707 FAX

Or browse online by series at:
www.peterlang.com